God's Great Story and You

Other Loyola Press Books by William A. Barry

Letting God Come Close: An Approach to the Ignatian Spiritual Exercises

A Friendship Like No Other: Experiencing God's Amazing Embrace

God's Passionate Desire

Here's My Heart, Here's My Hand: Living Fully in Friendship with God

Changed Heart, Changed World: The Transforming Freedom of Friendship with God

Praying the Truth: Deepening Your Friendship with God through Honest Prayer

An Invitation to Love: A Personal Retreat on the Great Commandment

Experiencing God in the Ordinary

God's Great Story and You

WILLIAM A. BARRY, SJ

LOYOLA PRESS.
A JESUIT MINISTRY
Chicago

LOYOLA PRESS.
A JESUIT MINISTRY

3441 N. Ashland Avenue
Chicago, Illinois 60657
(800) 621-1008
www.loyolapress.com

Imprimi Potest: Very Rev. John J. Cecero, SJ

Cover art credit: AngiePhotos/E+/Getty Images

ISBN: 978-0-8294-5430-7
Library of Congress Control Number: 2021933093

Printed in the United States of America.
21 22 23 24 25 26 27 28 29 30 Versa 10 9 8 7 6 5 4 3 2 1

For my beloved nieces and nephews
Mary Beth Knoeppel, Bill May, Michael May,
Steve May,
Helene May, and Matt May
and their families

Contents

Teach me to seek you,
and reveal yourself to me as I seek;
for unless you instruct me
I cannot seek you,
and unless you reveal yourself
I cannot find you.

Let me seek you in desiring you;
let me desire you in seeking you.
Let me find you in loving you;
let me love you in finding you. Amen

—St. Anselm of Canterbury

Foreword

Bill Barry was ninety years old when he died at the Jesuit infirmary at Campion Center in Weston, Massachusetts, shortly after handing in this book, his final one. He was a towering figure in Catholic spiritual circles, a pioneer in the practice of spiritual direction, and a revered spiritual master. What I, and our church, owe him is beyond measure.

And he has been with me, in a sense, from the moment I entered the Jesuits. When I was a first-year novice in the old New England Province in 1988, I had no idea how to pray. What was supposed to happen when I prayed? How did I start? At the peak of my frustration, a few days after I entered, the assistant novice director handed me a slim book with the title *God and You: Prayer as a Personal Relationship*. No single book has influenced my spiritual life so profoundly. It's not a stretch to say it changed my life.

The insight of this deceptively simple book is not only that God desires a relationship with us, but that a relationship with God can be fruitfully compared to a relationship with a friend. Using the same guidelines for what makes a good friendship will help you better understand, and deepen, your relationship with God. For example, if you tell your friend only what you think she wants to hear, the relationship will grow cold, distant, formal. Honesty is essential with God, as in any relationship. Insights like this unlocked prayer for me, and in the process, opened up my relationship with God.

In his long career as a Jesuit priest, Bill Barry was many things, all demonstrating the high regard in which he was held in the Society of Jesus and his native New England Province: assistant novice director, formation director, provincial and, finally, tertian director (in charge of the final stage of a Jesuit's formation).

But it was as a spiritual director, a teacher of spiritual direction, and an author on spirituality that Bill was best known. He was one of the founders and directors of the Center for Religious Development in Cambridge, Massachusetts, which for many years trained dozens of spiritual directors in the Ignatian way. His landmark book, co-authored with William J. Connolly, SJ, *The Practice of*

Spiritual Direction, is a classic in the genre and still used as a textbook in programs for spiritual directors. It is fair to say that Bill Barry is one of the main reasons for the growth in spiritual direction, the popularity of Ignatian spirituality, and the spread of individually directed retreats, in the wake of the Second Vatican Council.

But most of his many books, in addition to *God and You*, were written not for spiritual directors per se, but for a general audience. Their titles telegraph his main theme, that God desires a relationship with you: *God's Passionate Desire*, *A Friendship Like No Other*, *Letting God Come Close*, *Seek My Face*.

People often teased Bill that he wrote the same book over and over, but that was not true at all. Each book took a different approach to the topic (and some were more focused on things like the Spiritual Exercises and Ignatian spirituality), and in later years he filled them more with wonderful stories taken from the lives of his "directees" (anonymous of course) and his own life. His background as a psychologist also informed his books deeply. I find all of his books inviting, accessible, and frequently brilliant, and I cannot count the number of people to whom I've recommended them.

Bill's final book is now published by Loyola Press, his longtime publisher. I'm so grateful and happy that I was able to introduce Bill to Joe Durepos, the indefatigable former acquisitions editor at Loyola, which started Bill's long affiliation with Loyola.

Bill was also a great mentor to me, not simply as my superior but as an experienced author, reviewing nearly all my books and offering his wise advice and counsel. I treasured his insights and edits and corrections. And I learned a lot from him about how to write about prayer.

Over the past few years, Bill sent me the most generous, thoughtful notes and emails, supporting my ministry, complimenting me on a book or an article, or just to say that he was praying for me. I treasured his friendship and warm advice. During this past year, he reviewed my newest book, offering corrections and enhancements.

That new book, *Learning to Pray*, is dedicated to him, and I was happy that I was able to tell him that before he died. It reads: "For William A. Barry, SJ, whose books, and life, have helped countless people to pray."

When word came that Bill was failing, I was so moved to think of him finally encountering face-to-face the God whom he helped others meet in prayer for so many years.

For you, dear reader, enjoy this final work of a great spiritual master.

—James Martin, SJ

Prologue

On August 28, 1963, Martin Luther King electrified a crowd of over 200,000 people with his famous "I Have a Dream" speech. Even after the passage of fifty-eight years, his words stir the heart and bring tears to the eyes when they are heard on cassette or videotape or are read:

> I have a dream that one day this nation will rise up and live out the true meaning of its creed: "We hold these truths to be self-evident, that all men are created equal."
>
> I have a dream that one day on the red hills of Georgia the sons of former slaves and the sons of former slave owners will be able to sit down together at the table of brotherhood. . . . I have a dream that my four little children will one day live in a nation where they will not be judged by the color of their skin but by the content of their character.
>
> I have a dream.

In that speech, Dr. King was asking all Americans to join him in bringing about his dream. Many did, and in 1964 the Civil Rights Act was signed into law by President Lyndon Johnson. In this book I will be asking you, dear reader, to imagine God saying to you, "I have a dream; will you join me by helping me to bring it into being?"

When I began this book in March 2020, I whimsically gave it the title *Last Book* in my computer file. I had thought I was finished writing five or six years ago when I finished *Praying the Truth*. As it turned out, that was not the case. Two more have already appeared. But now with this one, I am almost certain I am done with writing.

I have the wild hope that with this book I can summarize the main ideas I have been peddling over the years in a new way that brings them all together. In short, with this book I want to help readers—you, that is—to know/love God better to have a more fulfilling and productive life. When I say "know/love," I mean to encounter God and to come to have a relationship of mutuality and friendship with God. By a fulfilling and productive life I mean a life as an image of God who is love, doing your bit to help further God's dream for our world. So this book will ask you to engage in some exercises of prayer and reflection that, I hope, will draw you into the kind of friendship God wants to have with you and with every human being God creates. So, be warned. This is not a book that will do much for you if you speed-read it. We don't make friends without spending time with them, as you know, a lot of time. So it is with friendship with God.

If you have read other books of mine, you may be saying, at this point, "But you've already done all this in a number of books. What's new about this one?" Well, I just finished reading a doctoral dissertation that gave me a deeper grasp of who God is and what God wants. Sister Ligita Ryliskyte, SJE, wrote the dissertation for her doctorate in theology at Boston College. The subject, "Why Was God Crucified?" will seem quite arcane to many readers. And truth to tell, reading it was, often enough, above my pay grade. But reading it did open my mind and heart to deeper comprehension of the mystery of God's love for us and moved me, at my advanced age, to consider writing this book.

I'm not going to take you through a course in theology, although theology will come into what I offer. I read theology now to deepen my knowledge/love of God and to help others move toward that same kind of knowledge/love. I am not a scholar trying to contribute to a particular field of knowledge, but a popularizer—that is, a writer—who tries to make what I have learned and experienced available to others so that they can profit from it as human beings and as Christians.

What I hope to convey to you and to engage you in is God's way of transforming evil and cycles of decline brought on by evil in our world. In Jesus, God was crucified because this was God's way of transforming evil at its root with nothing else but love. In other words, God transforms cycles of evil by remaining true to who God is, love. And God asks us to join him in this great adventure.

So, if you decide to take this ride with me, you will profit most if you take the time to reflect and pray, when it is suggested. When I suggest prayerful reflection or reading, we have inserted a little cross † as a symbol for pausing, reflection, and prayer. In addition, I think that you will be most helped if you take the book in the order in which it is written. As I envision the book's development, each section will build on the previous one. I follow the story of God's history with us, and I think reading the book from beginning to end, rather than haphazardly, will be most effective.

A word about prayer may be in order before we begin. By prayer I mean any way of conversing with God. That can mean laughing at some thought and sharing it with God or telling God how sad or angry or weary you are. It can mean asking God a question when you are perplexed or asking how God reacts to some event in your world that has affected you. Prayer doesn't even need words; you can just rest or cry with God the way you do with your friends. It can even be just looking at a lovely sunset or your spouse or baby and enjoying them as long as you know God is with you. So, when I ask you to read something prayerfully, all I mean is that you read it with God at your side, as it were, perhaps stopping at times to say something to or ask something of God. I hope this make sense to you. I have written two books on prayer that people have found helpful, *God and You: Prayer as a Personal Relationship* and *Praying the Truth*, in case you want to find out more.

I will be addressing you, the reader, often. I want you to know that when I write "you" I am including myself. The invitations of God are addressed to all of us humans, and all of us have fallen short, as St. Paul has written, in our response to God's invitations. In this book I am talking to myself as well as to you. We are all in this together.

A word about cycles of decline and of development. By these terms I mean what happens in and to our world as a result of our good actions as well as our sins and follies. How we act affects the world around us. And the effect keeps on giving, as it were. The reverberations of our actions through the years are what I mean by cycles of decline or of development. An example: When I was a senior in high school nearing graduation, a Xaverian Brother met me in a corridor and asked me, "What are you going to do after graduation?" I did not have a clue and said so. He said, "Why don't you go to college?" That kind question and suggestion set me on a track that led me to the Jesuits and where I am today. That brother did a good deed that started a cycle of development in my life that has had effects on many people. Another example: A father of two young children has an affair, and when his wife finds out, there is a loud and angry exchange between the two. The father leaves the family without talking to the children, and they never see him again. Both children have trouble in school, and the boy takes out his anger at the loss of his father by blaming the mother. When the boy grows up, he becomes estranged from both his mother and his sister and becomes an alcoholic. Here the cycle started by the father's infidelity has effects on the rest of the family that touch many other lives in an adverse way. That's how a cycle of decline is introduced into our world. Of course, in both examples the one who starts the cycle mentioned has also been affected by cycles of development and cycles of decline as they grew up. Does that make sense to you? You will read more about such cycles in the course of the book.

The general pattern of these chapters will be the introduction of a text or thought, the invitation to read it prayerfully for yourself, and then my presentation of further reflections. I believe it is important for you to interact with the material first in your own prayer and then consider what I have to say about it. The Holy Spirit is writing the story of the world and the story of you and me. Each of us is invited to participate—individually but also communally.

1

The Story Begins

As we begin this adventure, let's take a pointer from Ignatius by reflecting on the Trinitarian deliberation that led to the creation of the universe. Let's pause to ask God to draw us into closer relationship with him as we go on to reflect on what the Trinity intends by creating our universe and then by becoming one of us in Jesus of Nazareth. I believe that our understanding of the Incarnation will be broadened and deepened by reflecting on God's intention—or dream or hope—in creation.

The Trinity Sets the Stage: Creation Has a Purpose

Let's look at the first chapter of the book of Genesis to stimulate our imaginations. Neither of the two creation stories (Genesis 1:1—2:3 and 2:4–24) directly tells us why God creates, but the first does so indirectly, I believe. The author of Genesis 1 is trying to tell a story to indicate that God creates the universe from nothing, and out of love. Remember, it's a story, not an exact description of what happened; it is written not to give us facts but to draw us into that story so that we become part of what God intends with creation. I am suggesting that you try to enter the story imaginatively, first imagining the Trinity deciding to create, and then imagining creation. My hope, as was the hope of the writer of Genesis, is that you will become part of God's dream for our world.

Imagine God deciding to create a universe. What do you think motivates this decision? Why does God do it? Why don't you first ask God to help you imagine this story of creation from God's point of view? Then read the chapter slowly and prayerfully. When you have finished reading, reflect on your reactions to the reading. What touched you most? What gave you pause? What did you not understand? You may want to converse with God about your reactions and questions.

†

As you read that first chapter, did you notice how often it says, "And God saw that it was good?" Six times the writer makes that point, and then, after the creation of human beings, he writes, "God saw everything he had made, and indeed, it was very good" (Genesis 1:31). The number seven, by the way, indicates perfection; these seven repetitions are significant, as are the seven days of creation. Creation is God's perfect gem. Allow those words "and God saw that it was good" to touch your mind and heart. Doesn't the last one sound like the wow of a great artist who has just finished a labor of love and is overjoyed by how beautiful it is? Perhaps that's what the author of Genesis chapter one is trying to convey. What do you think? Let it sink in, and if you are inclined, talk to God about your reactions.

As I pondered this story of creation, I remembered the words of the First Letter of John, "God is love" (1 John 4:16b). I know that this letter was written centuries after the book of Genesis. However, the writer of the letter is reflecting on the same God depicted in Genesis 1. The writer of the First Letter of John is putting into words what has been true all along—namely, that God can be defined as love, period. God, who is love, creates because of that love. God desires the universe into existence because God is love, and with that same love desires that in the course of the evolution of the universe, human beings should come forth and flourish. Love is at the heart of all that is. The whole universe, with everything in it, is bound in a web of God's love. Spend some time pondering this truth.

Characters with a Part to Play: Made in God's Image

Let's reflect on the fact that God creates human beings in God's own image and likeness. "God created humankind in his image, in the image of God he created them; male and female he created them" (Genesis 1:27). Of course, God has only Godself to go by in creation. In a real sense, everything created is made in the image of God. But human beings are like God in their minds and hearts and thus must choose to act as images of God.

Maple trees and dogs don't get to choose how to act as maple trees and dogs; they just do what comes naturally, as it were. But it is our great fortune and our challenge that we have to choose to be images of God; very often, indeed, too often, we choose to act inhumanly, and thus are part of the problem of the universe, not part of God's dream for it. Yet, God chooses to make us in God's image and to trust us to cooperate intentionally with God in the development of the universe.

The grand story of the world begins with this fundamental reality: God loves us and trusts us so much that he wants us to be coworkers in bringing about the divine dream for our world. (I italicize that last sentence because it's central to the most salient points of this book. You will notice more such italics as we move on.) As you ponder prayerfully these scenes of creation, how are you reacting? Can you sense how much God loves you? It's very important for how we behave in the world to have a profound sense that we are loved by God. With that profound sense we will do more naturally what God intends. Without it we may try to imitate God, but we will fail because we do not have a real sense of who God is. Do you feel a deeper love for God and a desire to join God in this great adventure, this story of the world?

The Author's Driving Motivation: Our Friendship

Because we are given the gifts of intellect and will, we are capable of becoming God's friends. In fact, many great theologians believe that with these gifts God has made us for friendship—with God. Consider this statement: *God wants you to be God's friend.* A key aspect of the Trinity's deliberation about creating humans was the desire to invite us into friendship with God. What is your reaction when you dwell on this reality?

†

That last point leads me to suggest a prayerful reflection on the great mystery, only over centuries of reflection finally articulated, that God is relational in Godself. This Trinity-in-Unity is beyond our understanding. To get some grasp of the mystery, theologians have used the word "Persons" to indicate the three; but one has to be careful with how we understand the word "person" when talking about the Trinity. Also, theologians have said that the three "Persons" who are the one God can be distinguished only by their relations. But again we are left with the reality that we still do not understand the mystery.

I have begun to speculate that somehow or other we who are conscious images of God mirror the Trinity. Some modern philosophers, for example, John Macmurray and Maurice Blondel, have posited that human beings cannot be understood as isolated individuals but only by their relationships. Despite the individualism that permeates the culture of the United States and elsewhere, human beings cannot exist as human beings apart from relationships. "No man is an island," wrote John Donne long ago. You cannot conceive of a person without relationships. We need one another to be who we are. Perhaps this need for relationship is another way in which we are images of God.

I invite you to play with this image of the Trinity and your own life and being. Perhaps you will be moved to want to thank God for creating you in God's image and to thank those who have made you who you are. By the way, don't forget that you, too, have helped others become who they are. The positive effects of loving relationships reverberate in our lives down the years and so are part of the cycle of development God dreams for us. *Our relationships, especially our friendships, are mutual, not one-way streets, just as the Trinity's relationships are mutual.*

How does our friendship with God become mutual? After all, God needs nothing; the inner relationships of the Trinity are all that are necessary for God to be God and fully satisfied. This conundrum, however, vanishes if God, out of love, creates us for friendship, not only with one another but also with God. The truth is that God, strange as it may sound, wants our friendship. But because we are free, God can have our friendship only if we accept the offer of friendship. So, however it needs to be explained by theologians, once God creates human beings for friendship, God can receive something from us: our willingness to be God's friends. God can be, in some mysterious way, "disappointed" (and often is) by our refusal of the offer. When we do accept the offer, it must give him great joy, don't you think? That's what I have come to believe from my experience and that of others, even if I can't understand how it's possible for a mere creature to give God joy.

What does it mean that we can refuse God's friendship? God, in a sense, becomes vulnerable by creating us. Whenever we ask another to be a friend, we become vulnerable. Indeed, whenever we love someone, we become vulnerable. We are not in control of the other's response. Love and friendship are freely given, or they do not exist. Just as we humans take a chance when we love someone or ask someone to be a friend, God takes a chance on us. We wait for the other's response, and God waits for our response.

In her lovely poem "Annunciation," Denise Levertov writes, "God waited," as Mary ponders the angel's invitation to her. God invites every one of us humans into friendship, and then waits. *In creating us for friendship, God, in some real but mysterious way, makes himself vulnerable to us.*

One further thought. When we become someone's friend, it means that we take that friend as they are. A friend has other friends, and, as we grow in friendship, we come to know our friend's friends and, in the best scenario, become friends with our friend's friends. In fact, if I cannot accept one of my friend's closest friends, then I introduce a disturbance into my relationship with my friend. If I want to remove that disturbance, I need to change my attitude toward the person who is a close friend of my friend. And I may need God's help to change my attitude.

As friends of God, we are invited to become friends with all of God's friends. God invites us to widen our circle of friends to include God's friends wherever we meet them. *There are no boundaries limiting God's friends; friendship with God opens us up to a wider and wider circle of potential friends.* Because God loves the just and the unjust, the best saint and the worst sinner, we are left with the task of asking God to help us love all his friends, even the ones who are our "enemies." We may not be able, on our own, to love our enemies who are God's friends. If so, we can ask God's help to do so.

God's relentless desire for our friendship—and for our friendship within the human family—is the driving motivation behind the story of our world and us. We exist because of this desire. Every possibility for our lives is created by God's desire for us.

Where Are You in This Story?

God, who is Love itself, creates a universe that is good from its beginning (because God is good). Over time, human beings in the image and likeness of God evolve and take their place in this ongoing project of God. Endowed with intelligence and free will, we humans are invited to be God's friends and to cooperate consciously with God in the development of our world. If we accept this invitation, we will join God in creating cycles of good; we will be the source of actions that flow from love and that touch other people and the rest of creation. God wants the good created world to evolve as good, and we contribute to what God wants when we act as images of God. We help God create cycles of goodness.

The development God intends is a world where human beings live in friendship and harmony with God, with other human beings, and with the whole of creation. I have come to think that this harmonious universe is what Jesus meant by the "kingdom of God." Does this make sense to you? Does it square with your own deepest hopes and dreams?

Recently a friend, who was reading Iain Matthew's *The Impact of God: Soundings from St. John of the Cross*, remarked that St. John's spirituality was a tough spirituality. Out of the blue I said, "Have you ever thought of how tough the spirituality of the first chapter of Genesis is?" This chapter pulls no punches. After all, it tells us, in God's name, that we are made in the image and likeness of God *and* asked to be God's friends and cooperators in God's great project of creation. You can't get a more demanding spirituality than that, can you? Very few human beings have been up to the challenge throughout their lives. So, be warned, it's this spirituality that we will be praying and reflecting on in the course of this book.

But remember, God has entrusted us with this mission; therefore, God thinks that we are up to the challenge, even now. And the positive development of our world depends on how well we live up to the challenge. To return to our story metaphor, God's story is already in process, and we are invited to participate in the divine plot line.

I encourage you to spend some time reflecting on the story's beginning: creation. You might begin by noticing what is around you, all the gifts of creation. Enjoy the sun on your body; the sight of light filtering through some trees; birds singing; the taste of a fresh, crisp apple; the smell of a rose or a bouquet of flowers; the feel of fine cloth or the bark of a tree. Go on to imagine your family and friends and the things you enjoy with them. Think of all those events you enjoy, such as movies, concerts, music of every kind, etc. Everything we enjoy and that nourishes us in body and soul was created by God for us or by other human beings who were created in God's image. Any time spent on growing in love with God is time well spent, not just for our own sake, but also for the sake of the world, as, I hope, will become clearer as we go on.

These first steps, of experiencing God's love for you and of falling in love with God, are vitally important for all that will follow. If we try to live out God's magnificent storyline for us without knowing in our bones that God is in love with us, we will tend to take on the task of acting as an image of God as a burden and, even worse, believe that we can earn God's love by how we act. So, don't hurry on. Just as you have taken time to grow in love of your dearest friend, you need to take the time to grow in love with God.

2

The Great Conflict Emerges

It doesn't require a PhD to know that the world as we know it is not what God hoped for at the moment of creation. Just read a newspaper or view the nightly news. We are, as I write, in the midst of the COVID-19 pandemic, which is wreaking havoc all over the world, most especially among the poor. While we have seen numerous examples of selfless behavior, especially among those who work in hospitals, nursing homes, and marketplaces, we have also seen an outbreak of hoarding, infighting for critical supplies, and an unsavory willingness by some large corporations to take federal funding aimed at helping small businesses keep their employees on payroll. The enormous income inequalities both within the wealthier nations and between nations have exacerbated the effects of the pandemic on the poor and, here in the United States especially, on people of color.

In addition, in the United States the killing by police of yet another African American, George Floyd, led to numerous marches, most peaceful and some ending in riots. People continue to express their rage at what happened to Mr. Floyd and, indeed, at centuries of racial injustice. Unrest over these issues gives voice to the demand for reform in our culture and specifically in our ways of policing.

Even before the pandemic, it was clear that in many countries an unhealthy nationalism was taking root, along with xenophobic behavior toward immigrants seeking a better life or even fleeing for their lives. In the United States, our government had almost come to a standstill because of the bitterness between the two main political parties. These political gulfs showed themselves across the country. American political discourse is rife with hate and contempt. Things were so bad in 2019 that Arthur Brooks, former head of the conservative Washington, D.C., think tank the American Enterprise Institute, published a book titled *Love Your Enemies: How Decent People Can Save America from the Culture of Contempt.* "Culture of contempt" does capture the current climate of the United States.

In my lifetime the world has suffered one world war, and almost continual smaller wars between nations and civil wars within nations. The Second World War came despite the claim that the First World War was the war to end all wars. At the end of World War II, the United Nations was created; however, the United Nations has been dis-united almost from its beginning. War clearly only spawns more wars.

The Christian community has not been immune from the prevailing toxicity. Witness the vitriol with which almost every pronouncement by Pope Francis is greeted by some, especially online, and the corresponding vitriol spewed on those who condemn the pope. And, notwithstanding many ecumenical efforts over the years, the Christian churches are still scandalously divided, in contrast to Jesus' prayer for unity uttered in the seventeenth chapter of John's Gospel, just before he departed for the Garden of Gethsemane to be betrayed.

Stories of the Fall

In any authentic story, a major negative development threatens the good outcome everyone hopes for. God's great story of the world is no different. No doubt the world at the time of the writing of the book of Genesis was far from the good world God saw, as portrayed in Genesis 1. I presume that the story of the fall of the first man and woman in the garden aims to make some sense of the difference between the ideal and the real world. According to that story, the difference occurred because human beings turned their backs on God's offer of friendship. Let's reflect and pray on that story in chapter 3 of Genesis.

The second creation story, beginning at Genesis 2:4, is much different from Genesis 1. This is the story of the first man (Adam) and the first woman (Eve). I am aware that this story puts off many women. This part of the story has been used over the centuries to keep women subordinate to men. I would ask you to let that part of the story go and concentrate on the fact that the garden had everything the two needed. This story presents an ideal world created by God. There was just one prohibition: the two people could not eat of the fruit from the tree of good and evil.

Chapter 3 relates how Adam and Eve came to disobey that prohibition, thus ushering in the history of good and evil that still haunts humanity to this day. Remember that this is a story, not the report of a historical event. Try reading Genesis 3 prayerfully and noticing your reactions. You might want to talk with God about your reactions.

†

The serpent is clever, isn't he? *He insinuates that God has an agenda in prohibiting the eating of this tree, that God does not want human beings to be like God.* According to the serpent, God is quite the opposite of love. As readers of the Bible, we know, from the first and second chapters, that God has made Adam and Eve like God to invite them into friendship with him. The serpent wants to sow in their hearts a distrust of God, and he succeeds. This is how the cycle of decline from God's dream begins.

What happens after Adam and Eve eat of the tree gives us a sense of what their friendship with God was like. They hear God "walking in the garden at the time of the evening breeze" (Genesis 3:8). The writer appears to indicate God's regular practice, to sit down with them at the end of a day to chat about what has been going on. In other words, with this ritual the writer shows that God treats Adam and Eve as friends. This time, however, when God comes walking, Adam and Eve are not there. God waits and then calls out to Adam, "Where are you?" Here is an example of how God's love makes him vulnerable. God waits, like any lover, for the response of the beloved. As you think of God as vulnerable, waiting for our response, what is your own response?

†

The serpent tempts them to think that God is a rival who doesn't want them to realize that they are like God. It's crazy, but they fall for it. They now want life on their own terms, to be in control of what life has to offer; they don't want to be dependent on anyone, including God.

We have been created by God; so no matter what we do, we are always dependent on God's desire for us to be. We exist by God's good will, period. To deny this is to live in an unreal world. Crazy, isn't it? But we act crazily all the time, don't we? We all want to have control of our lives, but what we seek is an illusion.

Moreover, the serpent tells Adam and Eve that if they eat of this fruit, they will be like God. The deceiver hopes they will forget the truth of things: that they are already like God because God creates them in God's own image and likeness. *The tempter wants them to rebel against being like God at God's good pleasure, as if to say,*; "If you eat of this fruit, you will not need God in order to be like God." However, as they will find out, their idea of what it means to be like God will lead to some terrible consequences. *A cycle of decline—a falling away from what God intends—has entered Paradise.*

Almost immediately after eating the fruit, they find that they need to hide from each other and from God. Putting on clothes is symbolic of that hiding. Before eating, they were totally open with God and with each other, symbolized by not being concerned about their nakedness. Now, they hide from God and each other.

This is made explicit when they hide themselves upon hearing God walking in the garden at the close of the day. If you imagine that God made this a usual ritual of friendship, then you will also realize that they had no problem being naked with God before this. *We all know that friendships show their fragility when friends begin to have secrets from one another because they are afraid the friendship cannot withstand particular truths being revealed.* Thus Adam and Eve's friendship with God took on this fragility when they started to be drawn to the tempting words of the serpent.

Often enough in my life as a Jesuit priest, friend, and spiritual director, people have said to me that they don't need to tell God something of which they are ashamed since God knows it already. I have then explained that it's not a question of God's knowledge but of their trust in God. When they then begin to talk with God about this matter, they discover that they have a difficult time expressing it openly and honestly. Deep down they really are afraid that this matter could be the breaking point for God. *You see, it's not a matter of whether God knows the truth but whether we trust God's friendship enough to be open about the truth.*

Downward Cycles of Decline

As a result of losing their trust in God, Adam and Eve lose Eden, the good earth into which they were created. This loss of Eden is what the story is written to explain. Keep in mind that the purpose of the story is not to document historical facts but to recount and draw us into the larger story of humanity's life with God. This story of Eden and its loss is written to make sense of the real world into which all of us are born, a world in which human beings have become so inhuman in so many of their actions. *Evil has entered the world of God's good creation, and evil, once begun, keeps on rolling. A cycle of decline from what God wants has begun and continues to grow.* Another way to describe what happens is to say that, along with the cycle of development begun with God's creation, sin has introduced a cycle of decline in the flourishing of God's good world.

In the next few chapters of Genesis, chapters 4–11, we see the effects of this decline. Eve brings forth two sons, Cain and Abel. In a jealous rage, Cain kills Abel. In chapter 6 we read,

> And the Lord was sorry that he had made humankind on the earth, and it grieved him to his heart. So the Lord said, "I will blot out from the earth the human beings I have created—people together with animals and

> creeping things and birds of the air, for I am sorry that I have made them." (Genesis 6:6–7)

Noah, however, found favor in God's eyes. According to this story, humans and animals and birds were saved in the ark Noah built only because of Noah's fidelity to God. In chapter 11 we read that because humans built the tower of Babel, God confused their languages so that they could no longer understand one another, a story told to make sense of the disparity of languages that make it so difficult for humans to communicate with one another. At this point it seems that human beings have lost everything, including God's friendship, forever.

Take some time now to reflect on these stories. Do they tell you anything about the situations we face in today's world? Do you see any parallels or have any new insights into the state of our world? Do these stories, written so long ago, shed any light on our lives now? How did you feel when you read the words, "The Lord was sorry that he had made humankind on the earth, and it grieved him to his heart" (Genesis 6:6)? How would you feel if God felt this way about you or about your country? Perhaps you begin to see how these stories do draw us into the whole story of God's love affair with our universe, and with us humans in particular.

This story of what we call humanity's fall reveals that breaking our friendship with God has consequences. It's not necessarily that God punishes us; rather, the sins themselves have consequences, most of which we do not foresee. *Our sins contribute to the world's cycle of decline.*

Did you notice the blame shifting that happens in this tragic story? Adam blames Eve, and Eve blames the serpent. Something has gone awry with the relationship between Adam and Eve, hasn't it? They no longer trust each other as they did when Paradise began. Surely, this lack of trust played itself out on their children, perhaps leading to Cain's jealousy and murder of his brother. I don't know whether the writer of this story thought of Abel's murder as a consequence of his parents' sin, but as we imagine the story, we can make this assumption.

My hope is that you will get into the story and follow it through with your own imagination and insights. *As we do that, we get some idea of how we are contributing to the downward cycle that runs counter to what God wants. Our sins of commission and omission work against what God wants in our world.*

Where Are You in This Story?

As you ponder the third chapter of Genesis, reflect on its implications in your life here and now. Did Adam and Eve's hiding from God remind you of something that has happened to you? Did you remember some time when you felt it necessary to hide something from your closest friend and how you felt afterward? Have you tried to hide something from God? All of us have done shameful things, and we sometimes feel that revealing such things will cause others to abandon us.

You probably know from experience how such hiding causes a shift in friendship, a shift that makes the relationship less complete or honest. The thought of that lack of honesty can make you less free with your friend, for example, or it might make you a little more wary around that friend because you feel a needing to avoid that topic. It may cause a minor glitch in the relationship, but it could lead to a distancing between the two of you because you don't want him/her to find out that you did not trust that person at that time. This discomfort could lead to having to avoid even more topics because they come close to touching that sore point. Does this make sense to you? If it does, then you can see how lack of trust can eventually destroy a friendship. This is not what God hoped for in creating us.

Family disruptions result from mistrust among the members or from one powerful member deciding what the family should be like and ostracizing any members who do not conform. I know of one such family where the authoritarian father disapproved of the man one of his daughters married; he cut her off from any contact with him and with those loyal to him. Maybe you are reminded of situations like this. You can easily see how far from God's dream such families are.

Then there are feuds between families and clans. Something stirs up resentment between families, and the feud is carried down generations. Mention of such feuds reminds me of how within and between nations such feuds lead to continuous wars, sometimes lasting centuries. Witness how the former Yugoslavia, once freed from the Communist dictator who by force kept the disparate regions together, blew up into a savage war whose repercussions reverberate to this day. Ireland offers another example. When the southern part of Ireland won its independence from Great Britain in the early 1920s, a civil war broke out between those who accepted the peace treaty and those who did not. In Northern Ireland the ongoing feud has been between Roman Catholics and Protestants, both sides Christian and both Irish. The United States is beginning to have the same kind of internecine conflict between the Republicans and the Democrats.

Ask yourself if you have bought into the "culture of contempt" in the United States. For example, how did you react to President Trump and the Republican Party during the past few years? If you had a positive attitude toward them, how did you react when you heard Speaker Pelosi or Senator Schumer, both Democrats, speak? If you had a negative attitude toward the president, how did you react when you heard him? These questions may reveal that you, too, were caught up in the culture of contempt.

If you find that you do or did have some contempt for these politicians, please don't start on a guilt trip. All this means is that you are one of us humans, all of whom, as St. Paul has written, "have sinned and fall short of the glory of God" (Romans 3:23). The writer of Genesis did not write to have us wallow in guilt but to recognize the truth of things because of sin. In fact, God does not reveal to us our sins for any reason other than to bring us to repentance and return us to friendship with God.

If we continue to ponder, with God's help, the effects of sin, our gaze widens. We begin to see how the downward cycle grows ever bigger. We will note the terrible consequences of economic inequality in our world. The coronavirus pandemic brought this to light as never before. In the United States, the virus struck poor communities of color at a much higher rate than others. Why? Because of more crowded living arrangements and poorer medical care prior to the pandemic, and thus preexisting medical conditions among the poorest communities.

Just today, May 1, 2020, on the front page of the *New York Times*, I read that people in countries such as Bangladesh who had brought themselves out of abject poverty by working in garment factories (earning salaries of about thirty dollars a month no less) now had slid back into poverty because of lockdowns during the pandemic. The world has enough resources to feed everyone, but we do not feed everyone because the wealthier countries soak up so much of the world's goods. Does this make sense to you? Again, my purpose is not to make us feel impotent or guilty but to help us to see the reality of sin in our world.

What the frightful economic inequality in our world says to me is that we have lost a sense of belonging to one another as one family. Yet, the truth of things is that we *are* one family, if we take seriously the deep truth about humans conveyed in the first chapter of Genesis. Human sin does have terrible consequences as the cycle of decline keeps working in our world. One of those consequences, at present, is global warming, which threatens to destroy the planet that gives us life. Our reflections on our world have led us to the same place as the writer of Genesis at the end of chapter 11. Both scenarios bring up the question, Where is God now?

Where do you find yourself in the story of sin's downward cycles? How have those cycles affected your neighborhood, church, workplace, or family? When have you recognized the downward cycle, and how have you responded?

3

God Responds to Our Messed-Up Plot

Once believers in God become aware of the billions of years it took from the time of the big bang to the appearance of humans on this planet, they realize that God does not deal in time as we do. Fourteen billion years since the big bang that scientists believe was the beginning of our universe is hard for us to fathom. So when we try to comprehend how God deals with the effects of our sins and the messes these sins create, we have to reflect on a kind of patience and mystery that is totally beyond what we can conceive. Even though the story told in the first eleven chapters of Genesis speaks of generations, the actual time between the appearance of the first humans and the time indicated by the call of Abram in chapter 12 was very, very long. And, as we shall see, the way God deals with sin happens over a very long time.

God Chooses Companions for the Quest

In the story of Genesis up to chapter 12, God has been dealing with sin and its effects. For example, at the end of chapter 3 we read that God exiled Adam and Eve from Eden and laid punishments on them for their sins. However, he did not take back his offer of friendship. Throughout the following chapters until the end of chapter 11, God has similarly dealt with sins but has not revoked the offer of friendship. With chapter 12, however, a major turn is taken in God's dealings with us sinners.

When, as mentioned near the end of the last chapter, it seemed that at the Tower of Babel, God might wash his hands of us, in chapter 12 God creates a Chosen People by calling Abram and Sarai to leave the land of their origins and go where God will lead them. Thus began, according to the biblical story, the Israelites, the Chosen People of God from whom Jesus of Nazareth descended. Let's read it prayerfully together.

> Now the Lord said to Abram, "Go from your country and your kindred and your father's house to the land that I will show you. I will make of you a great nation, and I will bless you, and make your name great, so that you will be a blessing. I will bless those who bless you, and the one who curses you I will curse; and in you all the families of the earth shall be blessed."

> So Abram went, as the Lord had told him; and Lot went with him. Abram was seventy-five years old when he departed from Haran. Abram took his wife Sarai and his brother's son Lot, and all the possessions that they had gathered, and the persons whom they had acquired in Haran; and they set forth to go to the land of Canaan. When they had come to the land of Canaan, Abram passed through the land to the place at Shechem, to the oak of Moreh. At that time the Canaanites were in the land. Then the Lord appeared to Abram, and said, "To your offspring I will give this land." So he built there an altar to the Lord, who had appeared to him. From there he moved on to the hill country on the east of Bethel, and pitched his tent, with Bethel on the west and Ai on the east; and there he built an altar to the Lord and invoked the name of the Lord. (Genesis 12:1–8)

What stood out for you? What might you bring to your conversation with God right now? Go ahead and have that conversation. When you finish, you might be helped by considering prayerfully the reflections that follow.

What I notice every time I read this passage is that Abram drops everything and takes his wife and everything they own with him, traveling west toward Canaan, the land that now includes Israel, Jordan, and Palestine. He obeys without question. This blind obedience will not continue as his relationship with God deepens, as we shall see.

What also strikes me as important is the line "And in you all the families of the earth shall be blessed" (Genesis 12:3). *The choice of Abram and Sarai and all their descendants is not for their sake alone but for the sake of everyone on earth. God deals with the cycle of decline by calling a people from whom will come God's final answer to evil: Jesus.*

In their best moments, the Israelites never forgot this, but at times they, too, thought of themselves as better than others because they were chosen. Every so often they had to be reminded of their small beginnings. For example, in Deuteronomy we read,

> It was not because you were more numerous than any other people that the Lord set his heart on you and chose you—for you were the fewest of all peoples. It was because the Lord loved you and kept the oath that he swore to your ancestors, that the Lord has brought you out with a mighty hand, and redeemed you from the house of slavery, from the hand of Pharaoh king of Egypt. (Deuteronomy 7:7–8)

Let's not be too hard on the Israelites; we citizens of the United States have often acted as though we were exceptional, better than others. We need to heed this warning ourselves.

Companions Become Friends of God

I want to recall a few stories that indicate how Abram and Sarai grew into friendship with God. They were chosen to found a people, but for years this looked like an impossibility because Sarai was barren. In chapter 15, Abram complains to God that he has no offspring who will take on his heritage. God again promises that Abram will have a son by Sarai. Nothing, however, happens. Things become so desperate as both of them grow older that Sarai gives Abram her maid Hagar, who gives birth to a son, Ishmael (chapter 16). In chapter 17 God again appears to Abram and changes his name to Abraham and Sarai's to Sarah, thus signifying a greater intimacy and friendship with them. God goes on to say that Sarah, who is now eighty-nine years old, will bear a son from whom a line of kings will come. Then we read the following:

> Then Abraham fell on his face and laughed, and said to himself, "Can a child be born to a man who is a hundred years old? Can Sarah, who is ninety years old, bear a child?" And Abraham said to God, "O that Ishmael might live in your sight!" (Genesis 17:17–18)

Abraham laughed at God's silly promise and then said, in effect, "Get serious. The only son I will have is Ishmael. Bless him." Can you imagine yourself talking to God this way? Notice how God reacts:

> God said, "No, but your wife Sarah shall bear you a son, and you shall name him Isaac. I will establish my covenant with him as an everlasting covenant for his offspring after him. As for Ishmael, I have heard you; I will bless him and make him fruitful and exceedingly numerous; he shall be the father of twelve princes, and I will make him a great nation." (Genesis 17:19–20)

God still keeps to the promise about Sarah, but he also says that he will take care of Ishmael. By the way, how did you hear God say, "As for Ishmael, I have heard you?" I can imagine God smiling broadly as he says this. Can you? God seems to be enjoying this kind of friendly banter with Abraham.

In chapter 18 God again promises that Sarah will have a son "in due season," which we can assume means within the usual nine months. Sarah hears this in the tent and laughs. God says to Abraham, "Why did Sarah laugh?" to which Sarah replies, "I did not laugh" because she was afraid. God replied, "Oh yes, you did laugh." I imagine that God's remark here was also accompanied with a big smile, maybe even a laugh.

The call of the Chosen People, chosen for the sake of the world, begins with God forging an intimate friendship with Abraham and Sarah, a friendship that can even entail friendly banter. How do you react to these stories?

Immediately after this, God left Abraham and Sarah to see if things were as bad in Sodom and Gomorrah as God had heard. On the way God mused, "Shall I hide from Abraham what I am about to do, seeing that Abraham shall become a great and mighty nation, and all the nations of the earth shall be blessed in him? No, for I have chosen him" (Genesis 18:17–19). God then tells Abraham that he intends to destroy these cities if things are as bad as he has heard.

> Then Abraham came near and said, "Will you indeed sweep away the righteous with the wicked? Suppose there are fifty righteous within the city; will you then sweep away the place and not forgive it for the fifty righteous who are in it? Far be it from you to do such a thing, to slay the righteous with the wicked, so that the righteous fare as the wicked! Far be that from you! Shall not the Judge of all the earth do what is just?" (Genesis 18:23–25)

Can you imagine talking to God this way? In effect, Abraham tells God how to be God: "Shall not the Judge of all the earth do what is just?" By telling Abraham what he intends, God makes himself vulnerable to Abraham's reply. Would you dare to speak so straightforwardly to God? Now, notice how God reacted: "And the LORD said, 'If I find at Sodom fifty righteous in the city, I will forgive the whole place for their sake'" (18:26). This concession by God then led to a haggling session in which Abraham tried to see how low a number of righteous God will accept. Abraham stopped only when he got God to agree to spare the cities if there were ten righteous people there.

I remind you that no one was taking dictation. This is a story told down the centuries, and it was more than likely embellished with the telling. However, the writer of one of the most sacred texts of the Hebrew Bible did write this story, with its humor and its remarkable haggling at the end. He and the Israelites must have realized that their God wanted to have such a deep friendship with people that they could engage with God almost on equal terms and with humor. How does this affect the way you feel about God? What might you say to God now in response?

†

God deals with our sins and the cycles of decline they create by forgiving us and continuing to offer us his friendship. In the story of the Bible, Abraham and Sarah, friends of God, are the beginning of a new turn in the long, long saga of God's design to bring about God's dream of a world in which God and human beings live in friendship and harmony with one another and with the rest of creation.

Where Are You in This Story?

The stories of the Bible were written for the benefit of those of us coming after the time of these narratives. The writers, through their God-inspired wisdom, understood that the characters in these stories are human beings, like us. What happens to an Abraham or Sarah might happen to any person. These Bible-story lives reflect our own stories.

Can you look back on your own life story and see yourself as chosen by God to become a friend?

In reflecting on the development of Abraham and Sarah's friendship with God, do you see any aspects of their story that mirror yours, such as a call to follow God in faith, not knowing what would happen next?

Have you ever tried to tell God how to be God? Have you ever laughed at God out of disbelief, as Sarah did? Have you ever sensed God laughing at your foolishness or laughing with you in the natural banter of conversation?

How has God responded to your sins and messes?

4

God Forms a People and a Plan

Abraham and Sarah, as we saw, finally had a son to whom God gave the name Isaac, which means "he laughs." The writer must have meant to put this name in God's mouth to indicate God's sense of humor, because the naming of Isaac comes immediately after Abraham fell to the ground in laughter at the idea that he and Sarah could have a son at their advanced age.

Isaac married Rebekah, and they had twin sons, Esau and Jacob. Although Esau was the firstborn, Jacob tricked his blind and elderly father, Isaac, into giving him Esau's birthright. Jacob had twelve sons by various wives and concubines, and these sons were the founders of the twelve tribes of Israel, a name Jacob was given when he wrestled with God or an angel (see Genesis 32:22–32). If you were to read Jacob's story in Genesis, you would notice that while his trickery seems to have begun when he stole Esau's birthright, it did not leave him. Trickery was a factor in how he treated others and how others treated him.

Stories within the Story: The Joseph Saga

The stories of Jacob's twelve sons do not heap praise on them either. One of their terrible acts involved ten of them selling their younger brother Joseph into slavery in Egypt. I want to focus on this story because it touches on one of the major themes of this book: how God deals with evil.

Joseph was Jacob's favorite son, arousing jealousy among his older brothers. At one point, the ten oldest were tending the flocks at some distance from Jacob's tents when Jacob sent Joseph to them. As Joseph approached, they first decided to kill him and make it look as though he had been killed by a wild animal. One of the brothers, Reuben, prevailed on the others not to kill him but to put him in a cistern and leave him to die. When a caravan of Ishmaelites on their way to Egypt appeared, another brother suggested selling Joseph as a slave to them rather than leaving him to die. They agreed.

In Egypt, Joseph prospered and won the favor of the Pharaoh, eventually becoming the Pharaoh's right-hand man. It's a winding story, which you can read in Genesis chapters 39–41. Joseph interpreted one of Pharaoh's dreams as predicting seven years of abundant crops followed by seven years of famine. Pharaoh put Joseph in charge of storing up grain during the good years so that they would have enough in the years of famine. That famine also affected Jacob and his sons in Canaan. Here is where the story becomes quite interesting.

When Jacob heard that there was grain in Egypt, he sent his ten oldest sons there to beg for grain for their families back home. I would suggest that you now prayerfully read chapters 42–45 of Genesis. Note your reactions to the story and talk with God about them if you wish. Then come back to this chapter and the following reflections.

I hope that you enjoyed that very moving story. It's a strange story to tell about the origins of a people, isn't it? The only human hero is Joseph, and even he seems to want to take some vengeance on his brothers by forcing them to bring Benjamin, his beloved younger brother, back with them on their second trip to Egypt and by planting his own silver cup in Benjamin's sack. Do you know of any similar saga of a founding people that puts the founders in such a poor light? I don't. It's an indication that for the Israelites, in their best moments, the only hero is God, who chose them even though they were a tiny people with few heroes indeed.

Now let's reflect prayerfully on what happens in this story. No doubt, evil had entered the tents of Jacob's children, as was true in Jacob's own tent before his children were born. Jealousy took over the minds and hearts of the oldest ten brothers so that they could contemplate killing Joseph before selling him into slavery. *But God turned this terrible evil into a saving event in the history of Israel. God does not defeat evil by evil's means but by being true to who God is, Love itself.* That love manifested first in allowing the ten brothers to continue to live after what they had done, and then in watching over Joseph in Egypt. Moreover, Joseph's heart was moved to take pity on his brothers who had tried to kill him and to help them and his father even though he continued to hide his true identity from them. Finally, Joseph told them what the writer wants us to know about God's actions throughout this saga.

> Then Joseph said to his brothers, "Come closer to me." And they came closer. He said, "I am your brother Joseph, whom you sold into Egypt. And now do not be distressed, or angry with yourselves, because you sold me here; for God sent me before you to preserve life. For the famine has been in the land these two years; and there are five more years in which there will be neither ploughing nor harvest. God sent me before you to preserve for you a remnant on earth, and to keep alive

> for you many survivors. So it was not you who sent me here, but God; he has made me a father to Pharaoh, and lord of all his house and ruler over all the land of Egypt. Hurry and go up to my father and say to him, 'Thus says your son Joseph, God has made me lord of all Egypt; come down to me, do not delay. You shall settle in the land of Goshen, and you shall be near me, you and your children and your children's children, as well as your flocks, your herds, and all that you have. I will provide for you there—since there are five more years of famine to come—so that you and your household, and all that you have, will not come to poverty.' And now your eyes and the eyes of my brother Benjamin see that it is my own mouth that speaks to you. You must tell my father how greatly I am honored in Egypt, and all that you have seen. Hurry and bring my father down here." Then he fell upon his brother Benjamin's neck and wept, while Benjamin wept upon his neck. And he kissed all his brothers and wept upon them; and after that his brothers talked with him. (Genesis 45:4–15)

How do you react to this touching scene? Do you resonate with any part of it—any of the actions or words or characters? Feel free to stop reading and talk with God about this.

†

This story of Joseph is longer than most of the stories in the Bible. That length got me thinking that the writer wanted to make a special point about God and about his Chosen People. The Chosen People do not come off smelling like roses, do they? God is the hero in this long story, and God deals with evil as God alone, it seems, can. God transforms evil through love.

We need to be careful here. One way to read the lines "God sent me before you to preserve life" is to make God the perpetrator of the evil act—God wanted the brothers to sell their brother into slavery in Egypt to save the Israelites during a terrible famine. I do not believe this. I prefer to say that God allows evil to be done (without condoning it) but does not allow evil to have the last word.

What Joseph's brothers did was reprehensible, something that God did not want to happen. But God has made us free, and that freedom means that we can misuse it, and we very often do. This story tells us that God works to bring good out of evil. Joseph came into Egypt as a slave, but he was able to use his ingenuity and other gifts to win the favor of important people. Indeed, he became the savior of the Egyptians themselves at the time of the famine, as well as the savior of his family, including the ten brothers who had wanted him dead. Perhaps you may want to talk with God about your thoughts and feelings after reading this section.

I hope you noticed that God needed Joseph to forgive his brothers in order to transform the evil they perpetrated into good for all involved. If Joseph had refused to allow love to overcome his anger and resentment at his brothers, then the cycle of decline would just have continued in that extended family. God would have had to do something else to right the evil done. *But because Joseph forgave his brothers and invited them to join him and his family in Egypt to escape the famine, that cycle of decline, begun when the brothers grew jealous, was transformed into a cycle of good, or of movement toward what God dreams for our world.*

This story shows that God never gives up on us human beings becoming collaborators in God's great story of the world. This desire of God has repercussions for you and me and every other human being in the world. God cannot have what God wants in creation without our cooperation. *In order to overcome evil with love, God needs our help, just as he needed Joseph's.* How do you react to this statement? Does it scare you? Give you hope? Give you more desire to cooperate with God?

†

Joseph invited his father, Jacob, and his whole family to come live in Egypt since this famine promised to continue for a few more years. They made the move and settled in Goshen with the blessing of Pharaoh. Things went well for a long time, but by the time the book of Exodus takes up their story in Egypt, things have gone very badly for them. They became numerous and prosperous in this foreign land. A new Pharaoh feared that they would rebel against him if Egypt were attacked by an enemy. So he convinced his people to enslave the Israelites. Another cycle of decline has begun.

The Israelites' plight in Egypt kept getting worse; ultimately, Pharaoh ordered all male babies born to Israelite women to be killed. But the Israelite midwives often outwitted Pharaoh's minions and saved the lives of Israelite boys, one of whom was Moses. The infant Moses was put into a waterproof basket and left in the rushes of the Nile River. There the baby was found by a daughter of Pharaoh, who saved the baby and then gave him to his mother to nurse, without knowing that the woman was Moses's mother. After Moses was weaned, he was brought up by Pharaoh's daughter. Again God was at work trying to bring good out of evil.

More Companions: Moses and the Israelites

Moses's life story is told in the book of Exodus. When he grew up, he had to go into exile because he killed an Egyptian who was abusing an Israelite. While tending the sheep of his father-in-law, he saw a bush on fire, but the bush did not burn up. When Moses went to see it, God spoke to him, asking for his help in saving the people of Israel from their terrible slavery. God was moved by compassion for his people and wanted to save them but apparently needed help. Here is one part of that conversation, the one where God reveals the divine name. Let's read it prayerfully now.

> But Moses said to God, "If I come to the Israelites and say to them, 'The God of your ancestors has sent me to you,' and they ask me, 'What is his name? what shall I say to them?'" God said to Moses, "I AM WHO I AM." He said further, "Thus you shall say to the Israelites, 'I AM has sent me to you.'" God also said to Moses, "Thus you shall say to the Israelites, 'The LORD, the God of your ancestors, the God of Abraham, the God of Isaac, and the God of Jacob, has sent me to you'":
>
> "This is my name forever,
> and this is my title for all generations.
>
> Go and assemble the elders of Israel, and say to them, 'The LORD, the God of your ancestors, the God of Abraham, of Isaac, and of Jacob, has appeared to me, saying:

> I have given heed to you and to what has been done to you in Egypt. I declare that I will bring you up out of the misery of Egypt, to the land of the Canaanites, the Hittites, the Amorites, the Perizzites, the Hivites, and the Jebusites, a land flowing with milk and honey.'" (Exodus 3:13–17)

You may want to reflect and converse with God about your reactions and thoughts after reading this text.

This text is perhaps the most hallowed in the Hebrew Bible because God reveals the name God wants to be known by among the Israelites. The name, in the original Hebrew, is YHWH, a word connected with the verb that means "to be." Originally, Hebrew was written only in consonants; later scribes put in vowels. God's name, then, was YAHWEH, but it is not certain that these vowels were original. The Israelites were reluctant to say this name out loud; hence other names began to be used, such as Adonai, El Shaddai, or Elohim. In English translations, YHWH is set in capitals as in the above passage: "the LORD."

God was moved by compassion for the plight of the Israelites to make this intervention. God's friends, the Chosen People, were in deep trouble and needed to be rescued. I want to presume that you know the story of how God saved his people from slavery in Egypt and brought them into the desert. For my theme we do not need to rehearse that saga. What I do want to point out, however, is that Moses, like Abraham and Sarah, became God's friend and cooperator in helping the Israelites make it out of slavery in Egypt and into Canaan, the Promised Land.

Even in the text we just read, you will have noticed that Moses was a bit forward with God; he asked God to reveal God's name. God obliged. They have started on the path to friendship. Moreover, God asked Moses to take on this task. God respected Moses's freedom. God does not want automatons but friends.

The history of the United States gives us some idea of how difficult it is to get slave masters to give up their slaves. It took a civil war to free the African American slaves of our country. God did not want to put Moses into that danger without his consent. *But remember, God seems to need help to bring about what God wants. God is the author of this grand story, but we humans are characters with crucial parts to play. The story is incomplete otherwise.*

Let's move on to a later part of the story, the time in the desert. If you have read the story of the Israelites' desert years in Exodus, you know how fickle the people were, often wishing that they were back in Egypt, enjoying the leeks and onions and other foods of their time there, and forgetting the frightful conditions of slavery. At one point, Moses spent forty days on Mount Sinai with God, at the end of which God gave him the two tablets on which the Ten Commandments were etched.

While he was absent, the people got antsy and prevailed on Aaron, Moses's brother, to make a golden calf they could worship the way other people had their gods to worship. God was outraged and said to Moses, "I have seen this people, how stiff-necked they are. Now let me alone, so that my wrath may burn hot against them and I may consume them; and of you I will make a great nation" (Exodus 32:9). But Moses withstood him in the following words.

> O LORD, why does your wrath burn hot against your people, whom you brought out of the land of Egypt with great power and with a mighty hand? Why should the Egyptians say, "It was with evil intent that he brought them out to kill them in the mountains, and to consume them from the face of the earth?" Turn from your fierce wrath; change your mind and do not bring disaster on your people. Remember Abraham, Isaac, and Israel, your servants, how you swore to them by your own self, saying to them, "I will multiply your descendants like the stars of heaven, and all this land that I have promised I will

> give to your descendants, and they shall inherit it forever." (Exodus 32:11–13)

Then we read, "And the LORD changed his mind about the disaster that he planned to bring on his people" (32:14). Moses's intervention changed God's mind. That's the kind of friendship Moses now had with God. What do you think of this? How do you respond—emotionally and intellectually—to the idea of a person changing God's mind?

In the next chapter, God told Moses to leave this place and continue on their way to the Promised Land. God promised to send an angel along with them but refused to go with this people for fear that in anger God would consume them since they were such a stiff-necked people. Moses once again confronted God, who relented. Here is their exchange.

> Moses said to the LORD, "See, you have said to me, 'Bring up this people'; but you have not let me know whom you will send with me. Yet you have said, 'I know you by name, and you have also found favor in my sight. Now if I have found favor in your sight, show me your ways, so that I may know you and find favor in your sight. Consider too that this nation is your people.' He said, 'My presence will go with you, and I will give you rest.'" And he said to him, "If your presence will not

> go, do not carry us up from here. For how shall it be known that I have found favor in your sight, I and your people, unless you go with us? In this way, we shall be distinct, I and your people, from every people on the face of the earth."
>
> The LORD said to Moses, "I will do the very thing that you have asked; for you have found favor in my sight, and I know you by name." (Exodus 33:12–17)

Notice that Moses gave God two motives for coming with them—God's friendship with Moses, and the fact that "this nation is your people." Moses, like Abraham, was telling God how to be God, wasn't he? Does this kind of exchange give you some ideas of how to talk to God, your friend?

You may wonder where God's love for his people has gone as God contemplates destroying them. Remember that this is a story, not a recording. The writer is imagining God reacting this way. That God has not lost his love for his people, even though angry at their behavior, is shown by the fact that God did continue to accompany them into the Promised Land.

"Show me your glory" (Genesis 33:18) was the very next thing Moses said to God. Moses was cheeky enough with God now to ask for something for himself. He trusted God that much. And God agreed, although Moses cannot see God's face but only the back. The revelation takes place in the next chapter, 34. I suggest that you read it prayerfully and allow yourself some time to respond to God with whatever feelings or ideas arise.

†

> The LORD descended in the cloud and stood with him there, and proclaimed the name, "The LORD." The LORD passed before him, and proclaimed,
>
> "The LORD, the LORD,
> a God merciful and gracious,
> slow to anger,
> and abounding in steadfast love and faithfulness,
> keeping steadfast love for the thousandth generation,
> forgiving iniquity and transgression and sin,
> yet by no means clearing the guilty,
> but visiting the iniquity of the parents
> upon the children
> and the children's children,
> to the third and the fourth generation."
>
> And Moses quickly bowed his head toward the earth, and worshiped. He said, "If now I have found favor in your sight, O Lord, I pray, let the Lord go with us. Although this is a stiff-necked people, pardon our iniquity and our sin, and take us for your inheritance." (Exodus 34:5–11)

This passage is another of the great revelations of the Hebrew Bible. God's self-description is repeated a number of times in the following books of the Bible. The promise of visiting the iniquity of the children to the third and fourth generation is changed later in the Bible so that only the perpetrators of iniquity are punished, but the rest stands as God's self-description to this day. Because of the way Moses spoke with God, he was considered a friend of God who spoke to God face-to-face.

How do you react to these passages and to this kind of relationship with God? Would you like to have such a friendship with God? *I believe that this is what God offers to all of us. Not all of us, of course, will be called to lead a people out of slavery, but all of us are called to be God's friends and to cooperate in our own ways with God's great project in creation.* How do you react to that? Do you want to talk to God about your reactions? Go ahead.

An Important Character: The Law

When we think about the law of Moses, we often focus on its attention to details. However, as Antonio González points out in *God's Reign and the End of Empires*, much of the law is concerned with the kind of community Israel should be as God's people. Let's look prayerfully at some texts of the law to see what he means.

In Deuteronomy we read the following:

> When your children ask you in time to come, "What is the meaning of the decrees and the statutes and the ordinances that the LORD our God has commanded you?" then you shall say to your children, "We were Pharaoh's slaves in Egypt, but the LORD brought us out of Egypt with a mighty hand. The LORD displayed before our eyes great and awesome signs and wonders against Egypt, against Pharaoh and all his household. He brought us out from there in order to bring us in, to give us the land that he promised on oath to our ancestors. Then the LORD commanded us to observe all these statutes, to fear the LORD our God, for our lasting good, so as to keep us alive, as is now the case. If we diligently observe this entire commandment before the LORD our God, as he has commanded us, we will be in the right." (Deuteronomy 6:20–25)

Did you notice that the Lord asks the Israelites to tell their children their story? They were slaves in Egypt, and God brought them out of slavery. If the children understood this, they would realize that they, too, could still be slaves if God had not intervened. Also, the children are taught that the law is given to them so that they will no longer live as slaves but as a free people under God.

González goes on to show that many of the commandments of the law have to do with living as a community in which people care for one another without distinction and that tries to eliminate poverty as far as possible. Widows, orphans, servants, and foreigners living among them are often mentioned as needing special attention. Debts were to be pardoned every seven years (Deuteronomy 15:1–6). An Israelite should not charge interest on a loan to fellow Israelites (Deuteronomy 23:19–20). Land was to be returned to its original owner every fifty years (Leviticus 25:8–21). It seems that God wanted Israel to become an ideal community where no one was hungry, where, in effect, people took care of one another. Thus Israel's way of life would become attractive to other people who would see how well and harmoniously Israelites lived together.

What an attractive concept! What God wanted to develop among the Israelites was what Martin Luther King Jr. called the Beloved Community, a community in which love and justice prevail for everyone without exception. In such a community, cycles of love and development would be the norm. What is your response to such a concept?

†

Where Are You in This Story?

Throughout the book we will have to remember that we cannot live as isolated individuals, that we need one another and have to learn how to live in harmony with one another. As God's images we are asked not only to be individually moral but to become part of a community that itself mirrors God who is One-in-Three. At the time of Israel's freedom from slavery, God asked the Israelites to become a light to the nations by living as a beloved community. Not much has changed, has it? Our world is far from what God intends. We who are followers of Christ are being asked, as were the Israelites, to be light to the world in the way we live together and treat other people.

How do you react to the idea that you are a partner in God's plan for the world—that you are a character in the divine plot, or that God relies on human friends like you to keep the story moving in the right direction?

5

The Story Goes Wrong Again

Thus far, we have looked prayerfully at some of the earliest parts of the Bible to see what God intends with creation and how God deals with the cycles of evil and decline brought into the world by our unwillingness to live as images of God. I have been suggesting various stories from the first two books of the Bible for your prayerful reflection. I hope that you are growing in your love for God and in your friendship with God. *As noted earlier, and more than once, God creates us humans to be God's conscious friends and cooperators in the great work of bringing about the kingdom of God. We were created to be participants in God's great story of the world.*

Before we move on to another section of the Bible, I want to assure you that God's offer of friendship is actually for your good, as well as for the good of the world around you. Despite some rather dour images of Jesus and certain saints, what God offers really does lead to greater happiness and even joy. There's a sketch of Jesus laughing that you may have seen. I love it. We have already seen how humor plays a big part in the friendship of Abraham and Sarah with God. Those of us who cannot read the Hebrew Bible in its original language miss a great deal of the humor in it. What God is offering us is a way of life that will lead to our deep happiness, even if it goes against the grain of our own culture and perhaps every other culture that has existed. I hope you have experienced some of that happiness yourself, and I hope that happiness will grow as you deepen your friendship with God.

Disruption and Exile

The history of the Chosen People continued after they entered the Promised Land in much the same way as it had begun, with periods of loyalty to God interspersed with periods of infidelity. The one constant was God's steadfast love for them, even when God was exasperated at their infidelities. Some Israelites and their leaders and prophets stayed true to the covenant with God; many did not. *You could say that there are cycles of development and cycles of decline throughout the history of the Chosen People. God keeps trying to turn them from the cycles of decline toward cycles of development and uses faithful Israelites and others to assist in that effort.*

The great debacle in the history of Israel was the destruction of Jerusalem and the temple and the exile of many of the most skilled Israelites to Babylon in 587 BC. This was a shattering experience for the Israelites. The temple was the place where God dwelt among them. With its obliteration, it looked as though all their hopes and dreams for their country and themselves were destroyed. Finally, it seemed, God had had enough of their infidelities and was finished with them.

To get an idea of how devastating that first destruction of the temple was, remember that the only remaining wall of the second temple, destroyed in AD 70 by the Romans, is called the Wailing Wall. To this day, faithful Jews weep and pray and place prayers in the cracks of this wall. That gives us moderns a glimpse of the grief of the Israelites after the first temple was destroyed.

But God did not abandon them. The prophet Ezekiel was among the exiles to Babylon. He was relentless in detailing how much the Israelites deserved what had happened, but he also spoke of God's continued love and fidelity to the covenant. He did so in unforgettable visions, such as the raising of the dead bones to new life (chapter 37) and the glorious return of God to the rebuilt temple in Jerusalem (chapter 43).

In addition, the prophet known as Second Isaiah also appeared in Babylon (Isaiah chapters 40–55). He began his book with the great lines "Comfort, O comfort my people," used as the opening lines of Handel's *Messiah*. Let's ponder prayerfully some of Second Isaiah's prophesies, as a further movement in our deepening friendship with God.

Those words, *Comfort, O comfort my people*, were addressed to downtrodden and partially enslaved exiles who probably felt little hope of ever getting back to their homeland. God, however, has not abandoned them. He comforts them and tells them in touching images that the pathway back home will be smoothed. That pathway was largely desert.

> A voice cries out:
> "In the wilderness prepare the way of the Lord,
>   make straight in the desert a highway for our God.
> Every valley shall be lifted up,
>   and every mountain and hill be made low;
> the uneven ground shall become level,
>   and the rough places a plain.
> Then the glory of the Lord shall be revealed,
>   and all people shall see it together,

for the mouth of the Lord has spoken."
(Isaiah 40:3–5)

Can you imagine how these words affected the exiles? Their way home to Israel would be smoothed and easy because God would be with them. Have you ever felt dejected and deeply sad and then suddenly heard a comforting word that gave you hope and new life? If so, you can imagine how uplifted the Israelites in Babylon were by Isaiah's words, delivered to them as the very words of the God they had so deeply offended.

They must have been touched also by the following words of Second Isaiah:

But now thus says the Lord,
he who created you, O Jacob,
he who formed you, O Israel:
Do not fear, for I have redeemed you;
I have called you by name, you are mine.
When you pass through the waters, I will be
with you;
and through the rivers, they shall not
overwhelm you;
when you walk through fire you shall not be burned,
and the flame shall not consume you.
For I am the Lord your God,
the Holy One of Israel, your Savior.

I give Egypt as your ransom,
  Ethiopia and Seba in exchange for you.
Because you are precious in my sight,
  and honored, and I love you,
I give people in return for you,
  nations in exchange for your life.
Do not fear, for I am with you;
  I will bring your offspring from the east,
  and from the west I will gather you;
I will say to the north, "Give them up,"
  and to the south, "Do not withhold;
bring my sons from far away
  and my daughters from the end of the earth—
everyone who is called by my name,
  whom I created for my glory,
  whom I formed and made."
(Isaiah 43:1–7)

Wouldn't you like to hear God speak so tenderly to you? Many people down the ages have, indeed, listened to these words as directed to them and have been bowled over to realize how much God loved them, sinners though they were and are. How do you react to hearing God speak in this way to you? Perhaps you want to speak to God about your reactions and thoughts.

Let's reflect prayerfully on what is happening in these early chapters of Second Isaiah. The Israelites in exile knew that they were there because their leaders and, perhaps many of them, had not listened to prophets such as First Isaiah and Jeremiah. These prophets had strongly advised them against making an alliance with Egypt to save them from the armies of Assyria and later Babylon. They paid no attention to these warnings, and Egypt did not save them from Assyria or Babylon. Second Isaiah was there to remind them that God was still the God who appeared to Moses and declared himself to be

> a God merciful and gracious,
> slow to anger,
> and abounding in steadfast love and faithfulness,
> keeping steadfast love for the thousandth generation,
> forgiving iniquity and transgression and sin.
> (Exodus 34:6–7)

God's offer of friendship is not rescinded even when we, as the Israelites often did, spurn that offer and seek solace in places that take us far away from God. After all, it's God who makes the offer, and God, who is love, never changes, no matter what we do. What are your reactions as you allow these realities to sink into your mind and heart? Don't hesitate to turn those thoughts and emotions into spontaneous prayer.

†

Kings, Prophets, and Revelations

Throughout the Bible, even the Hebrew Bible, non-Jews feature as significant figures in God's story with his Chosen People. Just a few examples: Melchizedek, the king of Salem and priest of El Elyon, blesses Abram when he returns from a battle (Genesis 14:18–20). Moses is saved as a baby by the Egyptian daughter of Pharaoh (Exodus 2:5–10). Ruth, a Moabite who married one of the Israelite woman Naomi's sons, stays with Naomi after her husband's death, even when Naomi returns to Israel. There Ruth becomes the wife of Boaz and thus, the great-grandmother of King David (the book of Ruth). The Israelites believed that God used these foreigners as his cooperators in the development of the Chosen People.

Now, at the time of the Babylonian captivity, God, they believed, used Cyrus, the king of Persia, to bring their people back to the Promised Land. After defeating Babylon, Cyrus issued a decree not only allowing the exiles to return to their own land but also asking that his subordinate rulers help the exiles on their way with gifts and money, which they would need to rebuild Jerusalem and the temple (see Ezra 1:1–4).

Second Isaiah puts it rather strongly:

Thus says the Lord to his anointed, to Cyrus,
  whose right hand I have grasped
to subdue nations before him
  and strip kings of their robes,
to open doors before him—
  and the gates shall not be closed:
I will go before you
  and level the mountains,
I will break in pieces the doors of bronze
  and cut through the bars of iron,
I will give you the treasures of darkness
  and riches hidden in secret places,
so that you may know that it is I, the Lord,
  the God of Israel, who call you by your name.
For the sake of my servant Jacob,
  and Israel my chosen,
I call you by your name,
  I surname you, though you do not know me.
I am the Lord, and there is no other;
  besides me there is no god.
  I arm you, though you do not know me,
so that they may know, from the rising of the sun
  and from the west, that there is no one besides me;
  I am the Lord, and there is no other.
I form light and create darkness,
  I make weal and create woe;
  I the Lord do all these things.
(Isaiah 45:1–7)

Isaiah presumes that God speaks to Cyrus, a pagan king, and helps him in his conquering wars to bring about the release of the Israelite exiles from Babylon. I am more cautious in giving God credit for Cyrus's success in war, but I do believe that God deals with all that happens in the world and works in everything to bring about God's ultimate goal. I believe that God can and does move every human being toward acting as an image of God in what they do. So God does work with the Cyruses of this world (and everyone else) in order ultimately to bring about the kingdom of God. What do you think?

This point is important to remember as we move deeper into the mystery of God's great project of creation. *God is not a tribal God; God is the only God there is, the creator of all that exists, who chooses the Israelites not just for their sake but for the sake of the world.* What are your thoughts and emotions as you consider this?

At this point I want to introduce the four songs of Second Isaiah known as the Servant Songs (Isaiah 42:1–9; 49:1–9; 50:4–9; 52:13—53:12). It seems most likely that the writer believed that the servant was or will be Israel itself, the People of God. (There are other theories about who the servant represents.) Many Christians will recognize the last song because it is used in the liturgy for Good Friday. In this section I want to look at some of the themes of these songs as part of our ongoing prayerful reflection on who God is, what God wants, and how God wants to transform evil through love.

I have a fondness for the first Servant Song (Isaiah 42:1–9) because it figured prominently in a retreat I made many years ago. In this song, God is speaking about the servant. Let's read it prayerfully and then reflect on it.

> Here is my servant, whom I uphold,
>   my chosen, in whom my soul delights;
> I have put my spirit upon him;
>   he will bring forth justice to the nations.
> He will not cry or lift up his voice,
>   or make it heard in the street;
> a bruised reed he will not break,
>   and a dimly burning wick he will not quench;
>   he will faithfully bring forth justice.
> He will not grow faint or be crushed
>   until he has established justice in the earth;
>   and the coastlands wait for his teaching.
> (Isaiah 42:1–4)

As you reflect on this song, you may want to have a conversation with God about your reactions or questions. Go ahead.

†

God delights in the servant. Note that the servant will bring about God's justice in the world, but apparently he will do this gently and peacefully. If you look at the lines that follow, you will notice that God twice speaks of himself: "the LORD, / who created the heavens and stretched them out, / who spread out the earth and what comes from it, / who gives breath to the people upon it / and spirit to those who walk in it" (42:5); and "I am the LORD, that is my name; / my glory I give to no other, / nor my praise to idols" (42:8).

On the retreat I just mentioned, I felt that with these last words God was reminding Israel (and me) that God alone is God, as a hedge against pride on Israel's part and on my part. I began my retreat right after a difficult and painful meeting I had, as a Jesuit superior, with a group in a particular apostolic work. God was telling me, I concluded, that I was wanted by God, but not necessary. One evening, as I was walking outside the retreat house, this thought flashed through my mind: "You could be dead now." It was true; only the year before I had been treated for vocal-cord cancer, a form of cancer that, at that very time, was killing one of my first cousins. I broke out in a smile, thinking, *Somebody else would be superior. So why do you worry so much? You're not necessary*. How do you react to this Servant Song and my reflection on it? Perhaps you want to talk with God about your thoughts and feelings.

Now let's look at the third Servant Song (Isaiah 50:4–9). Why don't you read it prayerfully before we go on? Take your time reflecting, and talk to God if you are so moved.

Did you notice a new element introduced in this song? We begin to see why these songs are often called the suffering servant songs. The servant says, "I gave my back to those who struck me, / and my cheeks to those who pulled out the beard; / I did not hide my face from insult and spitting" (Isaiah 50:6). The next couple of verses continue this theme of suffering. Although the servant suffers, however, he also knows that God is on his side and will vindicate him.

The fourth Servant Song is a full-blown suffering servant song. I suggest that you read it prayerfully before we go on to reflect on it. You will find it in Isaiah 52:13—53:12. As you read, you will be reminded of hearing it at Good Friday liturgies or as part of the *Messiah* oratorio by Handel.

You may be moved to talk with God about your feelings and thoughts.

†

It's harrowing, isn't it? You can see why it has been used to grasp what happened to Jesus at his crucifixion. As far as I know, the theme of God's servant suffering in place of God's people is first heard in this song. I think that Jesus may well have been influenced by this song as he concluded that his mission was to die on a Roman cross as a way to inaugurate the kingdom of God. We are coming closer to the central theme of what God's love/friendship for us entails for God and how God deals with evil. Let's look more closely at some of the more salient themes.

The servant is marred beyond belief; his sufferings make him a source of mockery: "He had no form or majesty that we should look at him, / nothing in his appearance that we should desire him. / He was despised and rejected by others; / a man of suffering and acquainted with infirmity; / and as one from whom others hide their faces / he was despised, and we held him of no account" (Isaiah 53:2–3). I hope that you can see why this song was used to make some sense of what happened to Jesus on that Friday we call Good. Crucifixion was a torture devised by the Romans to degrade not only the people who were crucified but also what and who they represented. It was meant to make the crucified seem less than human, someone who could be tormented in this way to show who was in charge.

But the song introduces a new theme of vicarious suffering. The servant suffered these horrors for the sake of the people, as we hear in the following lines:

> Surely he has borne our infirmities
> and carried our diseases;
> yet we accounted him stricken,
> struck down by God, and afflicted.
> But he was wounded for our transgressions,
> crushed for our iniquities;
> upon him was the punishment that made us whole,
> and by his bruises we are healed.
> All we like sheep have gone astray;
> we have all turned to our own way,
> and the Lord has laid on him
> the iniquity of us all.
> (Isaiah 53:4–6)

This servant suffers not because of his own sins and failures but because of our transgressions and iniquities. The servant takes on the suffering we deserve. Remember that it is likely that for Second Isaiah the servant represents Israel, the People of God. So perhaps Isaiah, in this way, wants to explain the suffering that the Israelites as a people have undergone, especially at the time of the Babylonian captivity. Christians have, however, used this song to try to make sense of the crucifixion suffered by Jesus. *According to this interpretation, Jesus is the suffering servant who takes upon himself the punishment we deserve for our sins and iniquities.* Later we shall return to this theme when we reflect on the crucifixion of Jesus. How do you react to this section of the song and my reflections on it? It's possible that you are disturbed by this part of the song and its implications. You can have a conversation with God about your feelings.

When I write that Jesus takes upon himself the punishment we deserve, I do not mean that God wants him to suffer this punishment. I think that Jesus takes upon himself the consequences of our sins, the whole cumulative evil of the cycles of decline that we humans have brought into the world by our sins. We will reflect more on this point later in the book.

The next section introduces a new aspect of the sufferings of the servant, namely, that he undergoes these sufferings without resistance. Let's reflect prayerfully on this part.

> He was oppressed, and he was afflicted,
>   yet he did not open his mouth;
> like a lamb that is led to the slaughter,

and like a sheep that before its shearers is silent,
so he did not open his mouth.
By a perversion of justice he was taken away.
Who could have imagined his future?
For he was cut off from the land of the living,
stricken for the transgression of my people.
They made his grave with the wicked
and his tomb with the rich,
although he had done no violence,
and there was no deceit in his mouth.
(Isaiah 53:7–9)

The servant is clearly innocent of any wrongdoing; he does not deserve the punishment he undergoes. But he puts up no resistance, not even by word, let alone by an act of violence. This is something new in the Bible, I believe. Before this, the Israelites were encouraged to fight their adversaries with God at their side, and often fighting in their stead. Now, it seems, God asks this servant to suffer, without resistance, the punishment that we deserve. (Note that I am using the "we" that the song uses. Second Isaiah was writing not just for his contemporaries but also for those who would come after him, hence also for us.) *It seems to me that Second Isaiah sees God as loving his people so much that he will have his servant take on the punishment we deserve in the sense I just mentioned.* Perhaps you can see why Christians have seen in this song a prefiguring of what happened to Jesus. How do you react to this section and this reflection? Don't be afraid of any reaction you may have, even if it's revulsion that anyone would have to suffer in this way. I encourage you to talk to God about it, even if you don't like the reaction or what God asks this servant to undergo.

Where Are You in This Story?

The last section of the song (Isaiah 53:10–12) sums up the theme of the song and indicates the results of the servant's suffering for him and for the people of God. As we come to the end of this long section on the suffering servant, I would ask you to take some time before reading the next paragraph, imagining Jesus reading these songs in Isaiah, let's say in the early days of his public life, after he had run into opposition from the scribes and Pharisees. Ask him to tell you about his reactions to these songs. After you finish this contemplation, then come back to the next paragraph.

I hope that you were able to imagine Jesus reading the Servant Songs and were able to talk with him about what he experienced in reading them. If you did so, did you have any sense of how Jesus felt and what he thought? I hope you asked him about his thoughts and feelings as he read and talked with him about your own reactions.

As I contemplated Jesus reading these songs, I thought that this, perhaps, may not have been the first time Jesus read them. This time, however, was different because he now had more adult experience of communing with his Abba, his beloved Father, and of the dangers of his ministry. I felt that the songs resonated with his own experience of his Father's love for him and for his people. True, the songs unnerved him at first. What sane person would not have cringed at the thought of being treated as the servant was treated? But, I thought, he knew that God's love never changes, even in the face of evil. The servant's sufferings are evil and unjust, but somehow, Jesus believes, his Father wants to defeat evil by being true to who God is: Love itself. Jesus, I thought, had already become aware that violence begets only more violence; that, therefore, violence was a tactic of Satan, the enemy. The servant's nonresistance to suffering seemed to Jesus the way God faces evil—not that the servant, or Jesus, or the Father, wants this suffering, but that the suffering of the servant and of Jesus are the result of the cycles of evil introduced into our world by sin.

It seems to me that as Jesus prayed over these songs, he became more and more convinced that he, the long-awaited

Messiah, would need to follow the way of the servant described in them. As a human being he may not have been sure how evil would be defeated, but his Father would take care of that. I feel that, with some fear and trembling, Jesus came to see that he would be the suffering servant in order to bring about God's dream for the world.

How do you react to my experience of this contemplation? Does it give you pause? Make you angry? Begin to make some sense of these songs as referring to Jesus? Whatever your reactions, you can talk them over with Jesus and see what he has to say to you.

6

A New Major Character: Jesus of Nazareth

We ended chapter 5 by linking Jesus of Nazareth to the Servant Songs. In this chapter I want to open a prayerful reflection on Jesus' life and ministry as the Messiah. In the next chapter we will reflect on how, in his passion and death, Jesus became the suffering servant. As we continue the biblical story of God and creation, let's keep in mind why we have embarked on this journey. We have been asking God to help us to know who God is and wants to be for us and how God deals with the evil introduced into creation by human folly and sin.

Many people are not aware that the word *Christ* is a title. Often we seem to use it as Jesus' last name. *Christ* comes from the Greek translation of *Messiah*, the Hebrew word for "anointed one." The title clearly was not reserved for

Israelites. For example, Cyrus the Great, the king of Persia whom we met in the last chapter, was called the "anointed one" by Second Isaiah (see Isaiah 45:1) because he decreed that the exiled Israelites could return to their own land. In the centuries before Jesus, there arose a belief that God would send an "Anointed One," a Messiah, in the line of David, the king, who would usher in the unification of the tribes of Israel and the "world to come," the "kingdom of God."

In the century or so before and after Jesus' birth there was a strong sense that the Messiah would arrive very soon. Indeed, during these centuries a number of men proclaimed themselves or were proclaimed to be the Messiah, but nothing much came of them when, as often happened, they were put to death. Jesus' death by crucifixion should have quashed any belief that he was the Messiah, but that is not what happened. After his death he was seen alive by many of his disciples, and through their testimony and preaching, many more Jewish people came to believe in him as the Messiah. Rather early in the development of this group of Jewish believers in Jesus, Gentiles (non-Jews) also began to believe in him. Thus began what is now a worldwide, extremely diverse, multinational religion called Christianity.

Jesus of Nazareth entered our grand story. As the Messiah, he becomes the hero, the protagonist who will bring about the story's conclusion. But as you will see, he doesn't look or act like the heroes we're used to seeing in blockbuster movies or best-selling novels.

An Unlikely Messiah

I ask you to join me in the following prayerful reflections on Jesus. In this way we will come to know Jesus better and thus love him more ardently and follow him more closely. Indeed, as you begin each period of prayerful reflection, you might start by asking Jesus to reveal himself to you so that you will know him better, love him more, and follow him more closely. We can know another intimately only if the other reveals him- or herself. Once you have made this request, then read the text and let it touch your imagination and bring you into the story.

We know very little about Jesus' life before he was baptized by John the Baptist in the desert. His active work and ministry in the Holy Land may have lasted three years, beginning in his late twenties or early thirties. Consider this: God sends his Son to become the Messiah, the one who will usher in the kingdom of God, and Jesus spends twenty-eight to thirty years doing little more than growing up and working as a carpenter in a small village in Galilee, part of a very small country occupied by the Roman Empire. Then he had, at most, a mere three years of public life to accomplish what God intended, and that public life ended ignominiously in his crucifixion by the Romans. It doesn't make any sense, does it? If it hadn't happened like this, would anyone have ever thought of it as a winning strategy for God to pursue to save the world? Let the craziness of this sink in and then talk to God about your reactions and your questions.

Now look at the men he called to be his disciples. In Mark's Gospel, Jesus first called four fishermen who were throwing out their nets. They dropped everything and followed him. After a short while of gathering disciples, Jesus chose twelve whom he called apostles, "those sent," to be with him and to do the same ministry he was doing. Read the list in Mark 3:16–19. Most of these men are lost to history; in fact, the lists in the other Gospels do not agree on the names. Moreover, if we did not have these lists, most of these men would not be known by name at all. Is this the way to start the kingdom of God? "What is going on here?" you can hear the CEO of a corporation saying, "This is no way to run a successful enterprise."

But remember that the Israelites were told in Deuteronomy, "It was not because you were more numerous than any other people that the LORD set his heart on you and chose you—for you were the fewest of all peoples. It was because the LORD loved you and kept the oath that he swore to your ancestors" (Deuteronomy 7:7–8). What is your reaction to this statement?

Troubles and Danger

All the Gospels indicate that Jesus got into trouble with the leaders of his own religion rather early in his public life. In Mark, the trouble starts at the beginning of chapter 2, and the troubles fill that chapter and the beginning of chapter 3. At that point, Mark writes: "The Pharisees went out and immediately conspired with the Herodians against him, how to destroy him" (Mark 3:6). In Luke's Gospel, Jesus had just started his public ministry when he returned to Nazareth, the village where he grew up. In the synagogue Jesus read from the prophet Isaiah and then said, "Today this scripture has been fulfilled in your hearing"

(Luke 4:21). After this, some of the people started grumbling about him and then hustled him out of the village with the intent of throwing him off a hill to his death. He escaped. But again we see how early he got into trouble with the powers that be. Jesus lived a dangerous life almost from the beginning. Hardly a promising start for the Messiah, is it? God's ways are not our ways.

Despite the early opposition, Jesus began to draw large crowds wherever he went. He must have been a captivating speaker. He was clearly a wonder worker, giving sight to the blind and hearing to the deaf, curing lepers, even bringing back to life people who had died. In fact, the passage in Isaiah he read in the Nazareth synagogue spoke to the kind of ministry he was doing.

> The Spirit of the Lord is upon me,
> because he has anointed me
> to bring good news to the poor.
> He has sent me to proclaim release to the captives
> and recovery of sight to the blind,
> to let the oppressed go free,
> to proclaim the year of the Lord's favor.
> (Luke 4:18–19)

His ministry gave priority to those who were in trouble or on the margins of society. The crowds who followed him were not, for the most part, from the upper classes but were Galilean peasants who had to work hard for a living and had very little status or power. Jesus spoke to these poor people of a God who loved them and wanted them to be free.

Most of us probably don't imagine Jesus as a young man with a sense of humor and a love for life. Yet in the Gospels he seemed to get along very well with people of all walks of life, and especially with ordinary folks. Moreover, at one point he was derided because he ate and drank with sinners (see Luke 7:34). He must have been someone people enjoyed being with. We see his sense of humor in the nicknames he gave to some of the early apostles. He called Simon "Cephas" (Hebrew for "stone," translated as "Petros" in Greek); the late Daniel Harrington, SJ, noted that it probably should be translated as "Rocky," indicating something about Simon's personality. He also nicknamed James and John "Sons of 'Thunder.'" Perhaps Zebedee, their father, blew up in anger when Jesus pulled the two of them out of the family business.

I once read a scholar, name forgotten, who thought that Jesus' remark to the paralyzed man and his four companions who had just torn a hole in the roof of his home, "Son, your sins are forgiven," might have been said with a smile and a finger pointing to the hole (Mark 2:5). Also, when

I contemplate the story of Jesus and the rich man (see Mark 10:17–22), I sense that after the man says that he has obeyed the commands Jesus mentions (all of which have to do with our dealings with our neighbor), Jesus might have smiled to himself and said, "Oh, you've obeyed them all, eh? How about the first commandment?" before telling him, "You lack one thing; go, sell what you own, and give the money to the poor, and you will have treasure in heaven; then come, follow me" (10:21).

I suggest that you keep in mind Jesus' humor when you read the Gospels. You might be surprised and find him much more approachable than you thought. You might find that he's the kind of person you would like to chat with over a beer or coffee.

Jesus was a great teacher who taught not only by word and story but especially by action. The Gospels often speak of his compassion, a strong emotional response often attributed to God in the Hebrew Bible.

In Mark's first chapter, for example, we read, "A leper came to him begging him, and kneeling he said to him, 'If you choose, you can make me clean.' Moved with pity, Jesus stretched out his hand and touched him, and said to him, 'I do choose. Be made clean!' Immediately the leprosy left him, and he was made clean" (Mark 1:40–42).

The word translated as "pity" here is the same word used to translate the Hebrew word for compassion in the Greek translation of the Hebrew Bible. This is only one of many such instances in the Gospels where Jesus' compassion is noted. Jesus acted as God acts; he was, like the rest of us human beings, an image of God when he acted with compassion, but he was the Son of God.

In the Hebrew Bible, God is frequently depicted as on the side of the widow, the outcast, and the alien. Jesus often showed himself on the side of the outcast, as in his cure of this leper. He was known as someone who ate with sinners and outcasts, such as tax collectors. When attacked for this behavior, he noted that he had come not to save the righteous but sinners.

When, at a wedding feast in Cana, Jesus' mother told him that they had no more wine, he changed an enormous amount of water into a very fine wine for the party (see John 2:1–11). That must have been a great party. Here he showed in action that with his coming the Messianic banquet had begun. It was time to celebrate.

He cured the sick, gave sight to the blind and hearing to the deaf, and even raised some people from the dead. By these actions Jesus demonstrated that the kingdom of God had entered this world with him.

The final great action, of course, was his death on a Roman cross. We will come back to that in the next chapter.

With all his actions, Jesus demonstrated that it is possible as a human being to be an image of God. You might object, "But he was God." Such thinking can be used to get us off the hook. We have to keep in mind, all the time, that Jesus was a human being, like us in all things except sin. This is the scandal of Jesus, actually. He is the Son of God, but he was also a human being who needed to be toilet-trained and to learn a language as a child, who had to learn how to live in this world, who had to figure out his calling in life like anyone else.

We tend to have some ideas of what it means to be God, and then we plaster those ideas onto Jesus. The result is that, for many of us, he only looks like a human being but is really God. This is the heresy of Docetism, which was condemned in the early church but which lives with us still. I recall reading a remark of the great German theologian, Karl Rahner, SJ, that most Christians were Docetists, thinking, "Wasn't it nice of the good God to come among us looking like a human being?" Let's try to take seriously that Jesus was a real human being like us. He learned how to live as an image of God as an adult. He seems to have thought that we could do the same thing. In fact, he put his whole life on the line to save us from our unwillingness to be images of God.

How do you respond to Jesus' way of being the Messiah? How do you respond to his choice of company, his tendency to get into trouble? Talk with God about this.

The Storyteller and Teacher

Jesus was a great storyteller who used this gift to get his points across. I think he would have agreed with those who say that if you want to change people's minds, tell them a story. The Gospel of Luke is a treasure trove of Jesus' stories. Here's a partial list that you can look up sometime: Luke 7:36–50 (the story is embedded within this event in Jesus' life); 8:4–18 (scattering of seed and lighting a lamp); 10:25–37 (the Good Samaritan); 11:5–13 (the importunate neighbor and the good father); 12:16–21 (the rich fool); 14:16–24 (invitation to a large dinner party); 15:1–32 (one lost sheep, one lost small coin, the prodigal son); 16:19–31 (the rich man and Lazarus); 18:9–14 (the Pharisee and the tax collector). Let's look at only a couple of these stories to see how Jesus, through a story, gets across something about who God is.

We begin with the prodigal son because Jesus uses it to illustrate how to act like a person made in God's image, even when attacked. The opening lines of chapter 15 set the scene: "Now all the tax-collectors and sinners were coming near to listen to him. And the Pharisees and the scribes were grumbling and saying, 'This fellow welcomes sinners and eats with them'" (Luke 15:1–2). By his action in welcoming the outcasts and eating with them, Jesus offended the Pharisees and scribes. They believed that God rejects such people; hence, all good Jews should have nothing to do with them. Jesus did not get into an argument with them about God; rather he told three stories: the lost sheep, the lost coin, and the lost prodigal son. Let's look prayerfully at the last story because it reveals so much about who God is. Please take your Bible and read Luke 15:11–32, slowly and prayerfully. Pay attention to your reactions. You might even write them down and talk with Jesus about them.

It's a brilliant story, isn't it? Jesus must have had the audience hanging on his every word. I doubt that the Pharisees and scribes were enthralled; they must have sensed by the time this third story came along that they were between a rock and a hard place in this argument with Jesus. Anyone listening to the story will recognize immediately that the father represents God. And they will recognize as immediately that this father is not like many human fathers.

Most fathers at that time (and still, perhaps) would have been insulted and angry at the younger son right from his first request; after all, the son was saying in effect, "I wish you were dead." Sons got their inheritance only at the death of their father. But this father quickly gave the young man his inheritance, after which the son ran off with the money to waste it on wild living. Isn't this the God we've been meeting throughout the book, who gives us our inheritance—to be images of God—and hopes that we will act as such? In that culture, and in many others to this day, the son's behavior was a black mark on the family, especially the father. The whole village would get wind of what happened and how low the son had sunk, feeding pigs for a Gentile; to Jews, pigs were considered nasty and unclean.

As you read the story, did you notice that the father saw the son at a distance? Perhaps the father often looked into the distance to see if his son was coming home. It's a touching image of God, isn't it? As I read it, I was reminded of how God makes himself vulnerable by loving us. Here the father waited in hope for his son's return, just as God waited for Mary's yes to being the mother of Jesus and waits for us to accept his offer of friendship. Then the father ran through the village to throw his arms around the wastrel, an even more touching image that shows how much God yearns for the return of sinners.

Did you imagine how the young man looked and smelled? Remember that he had just left a pig sty in haste because he was so hungry. I doubt that he had the time or place to clean up before returning. What do you think? I imagine the son reeking as his father embraced him. But the father did not flinch, nor did he hesitate to order his servants to get the young man cleaned up and dressed in good clothes for, of all things, a big banquet. This father wanted the whole village to rejoice with him that his son had come back. Doesn't Jesus paint an attractive and touching image of his Father?

It becomes even more touching when the older son refused to come in, even refusing to call this son his brother. "This son of yours," he yelled at their father. This son expressed the resentment that had built over the years. Notice how the father, in Jesus' story, handled this angry barrage. Instead of returning anger for anger, he spoke tenderly to him: "Son, you are always with me, and all that is mine is yours. But we had to celebrate and rejoice, because this brother of yours was dead and has come to life; he was lost and has been found" (Luke 15:32).

Ponder for a moment the power of those words from the father: "Son, you are always with me." Then the father showed how much he loved him and expected of him by reminding him that it was his brother who was dead and had come to life, was lost and had been found. The father wanted this son to have a change of heart toward his brother so that they were again one family. That's my way of finishing the story. I believe that this kind of reconciliation is what God wants for all of us. *If my sense of the ending is correct, then the end of the story reinforces the idea that God transforms evil through love; both sons are brought back into the family, creating a cycle of positive development in the family.*

Some commentators think that Jesus might be hinting to the Pharisees and scribes that they were acting like the older brother. If so, then the tender way the father dealt with the older son might well indicate that Jesus himself harbored only love for the Pharisees and scribes who were attacking him. This might be another aspect of the story that speaks of how all-embracing God's love is. Given what happens to Jesus at the end of his life, it seems that his love for his enemies did not always win out, at least in the short run, but, like his Father, he never stops loving.

Now let's turn to the Good Samaritan story, reading it prayerfully and asking Jesus to help us get his point about God and neighbor. You will find it in your Bible in Luke's Gospel 10:25–37.

In Luke's telling, the lawyer was hostile from the beginning. Jesus did not respond in anger. He asked the lawyer to interpret the law and then commended his answer. Then, when the lawyer still wanted an argument, Jesus did not respond in kind but told a great story that resonates to this day. (In the United States, and perhaps in other countries, there is an organization called the Samaritans whose members are on call for those who are contemplating suicide. The name of the organization is a clear reference to this story.)

I presume that the mugged man was a Jew who was going from Jerusalem to Jericho, perhaps after worshipping at the temple. This road was known as dangerous, and our traveler experienced the fate of many who traveled the road alone. As he lay there, Jesus tells us, three people saw him. The first two walked on the other side of the road so as not to come too close to him. The third man was a Samaritan, someone who was considered an enemy of the Jewish people.

Jesus says that the Samaritan was moved with compassion ("pity" in this NRSV translation) and acted on that compassion, taking care of the man and then taking him to an inn and paying for his stay, even promising the innkeeper that he would come back to pay for any expenses incurred over and above what he had given him. *The Samaritan acts as an image of the God of compassion.*

Then Jesus clinched the point of the story by asking the lawyer, in effect, whom he would want as a neighbor if he were that mugged man. Jesus turns the question from "Who is my neighbor?" to "Who would I want as a neighbor if I were in trouble?" That question hits home to all of us, doesn't it? I would not care what nationality, what race, or what religion a passerby might be as long as that person helped me when I needed it. Jesus says to each of us, "Go and do likewise. Be a neighbor to anyone in trouble, if it's at all possible."

Behind the message of this great story, of course, is that we are images of God who shows love and compassion to everyone. Jesus, once again, is telling us that God wants us to help him in caring for all human beings and, indeed, all creatures.

How do you react to this story and my reflections on it? No matter what your reactions, you will have something to talk about with Jesus. I would encourage you to read the story with your own version of the three passersby, perhaps including either a person or a group of people you don't like as the Samaritan. If you find that you can't have compassion for certain people, for whatever reason, including bias, just talk with Jesus about your difficulty. You can tell him that you can't be a neighbor to someone and ask him if you can still keep talking with him, or you can ask him to help you change your attitude toward that person. There is never a good reason to stop talking with God about a difficult problem.

†

I can't leave this section of stories without mentioning the great story of the Last Judgment in Matthew 25:31–46. I leave this to your own prayer and reflection, only noting that in the story the way we treat others is equated with the way we treat Jesus. That's how closely God and human beings are entwined.

Jesus was also known as a teacher. In fact, Matthew's Gospel has five long sections of teaching (5:1—7:29; 9:35—11:1; 13:2–52; 18:1–35; 24:1—25:46). Moses was considered the author of the first five books of the Bible, collectively called the Pentateuch. By collecting these five sets of Jesus' teachings together in this way, Matthew shows

Jesus as the new Moses teaching the People of God, which now includes people of the whole world. In these five sets of teachings Jesus often uses parables or stories to make his points. In this section I want to focus our attention on parts of the first great set of teachings, known as the Sermon on the Mount, because the teachings touch directly on the main theme we have been developing in this book, who God is, what God hopes for from us humans, and how God deals with evil in the world.

Let's start at the beginning with what are usually called the Beatitudes. The usual translation of each of these beatitudes is "blessed are. . . ." Several translations use "happy" for the Greek "Makarios," including N.T. Wright's *Matthew for Everyone*, and the *Common English Bible*. I want to use the latter translation here because it may give us a new and different take on what Jesus is getting at. Once again, I ask you to read the following text prayerfully and to spend some time reflecting on what you have read and, if so moved, in conversing with Jesus about what he has said.

> Happy are people who are hopeless, because the
> kingdom of heaven is theirs.
> Happy are people who grieve, because they will be
> made glad.
> Happy are people who are humble, because they will
> inherit the earth.

> Happy are people who are hungry and thirsty for righteousness, because they will be fed until they are full.
> Happy are people who show mercy, because they will receive mercy.
> Happy are people who have pure hearts, because they will see God.
> Happy are people who make peace, because they will be called God's children.
> Happy are people whose lives are harassed because they are righteous, because the kingdom of heaven is theirs.
> Happy are you when people insult you and harass you and speak all kinds of bad and false things about you, all because of me. Be full of joy and be glad, because you have a great reward in heaven. In the same way, people harassed the prophets who came before you.
> (Matthew 5:3–12, CEB).

Did it strike you as strange to hear Jesus say that the hopeless, the grieving, the humble, and especially those who are treated shabbily, even harshly, by others are happy? Perhaps Jesus wanted to startle his listeners and all those who would later hear these beatitudes. So, if you are startled, even flabbergasted, welcome to the club. The kingdom of

God ("of heaven" in Matthew) because he was writing for a Jewish-Christian audience who might be put off by the use of God's name) is, big-time, different from the world we live in and even expect. Yet these Beatitudes begin one of the largest sections of teachings in Matthew's Gospel. Jesus must be serious. Let's reflect prayerfully on the deeper meaning of the Beatitudes.

Jesus, here, was teaching disciples who had only recently joined his movement. He wanted them to know what they were getting into. As the long-awaited Messiah he was ushering in the final stage of the world God has wanted from its beginning. Jesus called this final stage the kingdom of God, a world where everyone will live in harmony with God, with one another, and with the whole of creation. They (and we) are being asked to live as though this world were already in full swing. If they do live as though the kingdom is present, Jesus says, they will be happy, no matter what it looks like to others. Not only that, but they will be helping God to bring about the kingdom of God. *Here's another way to put what Jesus is saying: "Try living as though the kingdom were already existing. You'll never regret it. You will be very happy."*

The late congressman John Lewis told the author and radio host Krista Tippett how, as a young man, he joined the movement started by Martin Luther King Jr., a movement that used the tactics of nonviolent resistance to gain civil rights for African Americans. Lewis describes how that movement brought together African Americans and white Americans who tried to live as though the Beloved Community already were in existence.[1]

I'm trying to put into words something that is mysterious and, therefore, hard to grasp. I'm groping, as you may be. Jesus often used stories to make his points, but he had to have some human understanding of what he wanted to get across with the stories. I am trying to grasp something of that human understanding—so that you and I can live it out.

Right after the Beatitudes, Jesus tells his disciples (and us) that they are the salt of the earth and the light of the world. We are being asked to live now as the images of God we are created to be and in this way to be part of the great cycle of love begun by Jesus. We are asked to help God to bring about God's dream for our world, a dream that God had before the beginning of time. In the rest of the Sermon on the Mount, Jesus gives pointers on the kinds of behaviors the kingdom needs from us.

Many of these pointers, especially in the rest of Matthew chapter 5, indicate that Jesus is the new Moses, reinterpreting the law. They have a form like this: "You have heard that it was said . . . but I say to you . . ." However, before he gets into these reinterpretations, Jesus pointedly says, "Do not think that I have come to abolish the law or the prophets; I have come not to abolish but to fulfill. For truly I tell you, until heaven and earth pass away, not one letter, not one stroke of a letter, will pass from the law until all is accomplished" (Matthew 5:17–18). Jesus was a faithful Jew and remained so to the end of his life.

Now to some of the pointers. He brings up the commandment against murder and then says, "But I say to you that if you are angry with a brother or sister, you will be liable to judgment; and if you insult a brother or sister, you will be liable to the council; and if you say, 'You fool,' you will be liable to the hell of fire" (Matthew 5:22). Murder is not the only way to injure others; for Jesus, calling them names and otherwise insulting them is just as bad.

How does that sit with you? If you think about it, I'm sure you will see that such behaviors destroy the kind of harmony and love that should prevail among us in the kingdom of God. If that is so, Jesus says, put it into practice now. In the same way he notes that the commandments forbid adultery, but he adds that any lustful looks or thoughts are just as harmful in the kingdom of God. Such actions demean others and make them sex objects, not brothers or sisters in the Lord.

Jesus brings up the law of retaliation, an eye for an eye and a tooth for a tooth, and then says,

> But I say to you, Do not resist an evildoer. But if anyone strikes you on the right cheek, turn the other also; and if anyone wants to sue you and take your coat, give your cloak as well; and if anyone forces you to go one mile, go also the second mile. Give to everyone who begs from you, and do not refuse anyone who wants to borrow from you. (Matthew 5:39–42)

It's getting a little uncomfortable, isn't it? Jesus is not offering a spirituality that merely comforts; it also challenges us, and at the deepest levels of our hearts. A Jew listening to this injunction would most likely think of the Roman occupiers of his country as the attackers.

By the way, think of what our world would be like if the law of strict retaliation ("an eye for an eye, a tooth for a tooth") were fully enforced. Eventually no one would be able to see or eat. It would be the very opposite of the kingdom of God, wouldn't it? No one could trust anyone else; everyone would have to look out for him/herself. That's how a cycle of decline works; it finally leads to a nightmare world indeed.

I remind you (and me) that if you find it impossible to go the extra mile, you are not alone; most of us cannot do it. However we can always tell God that we cannot do it—or even don't want to do it—and ask for help, both to want to do it and to do it. We are never alone in the struggle to live as images of God. God has promised one thing, to be with us always until the end of time.

The next pointer is even more difficult. Take some time reflecting prayerfully on this last section of chapter 5 of Matthew. Jesus starts by saying that one interpretation of the law says, "You shall love your neighbor and hate your enemy." He then says,

> But I say to you, Love your enemies and pray for those who persecute you, so that you may be children of your Father in heaven; for he makes his sun rise on the evil and on the good, and sends rain on the righteous and on the unrighteous. For if you love those who love you, what reward do you have? Do not even the tax collectors do the same? And if you greet only your brothers and sisters, what more are you doing than others? Do not even the Gentiles do the same? Be perfect, therefore, as your heavenly Father is perfect. (Matthew 5:43–48)

Jesus not only tells us how to act with enemies but also gives the motivation. The substance is, Do what God does.

As you probably expect by now, I was taken by the reference to God at the beginning and the end. God helps out the evil and the good people of this world; all are God's beloved. And we are enjoined to act as God acts. The Greek word translated "perfect" in this NRSV translation can also be translated "complete." Jesus seems to be saying that God's ethical standards are the highest; since we are made in the image and likeness of God, we, too, are asked to aim that high. No doubt it is a very high standard. However, look at what holding to the older interpretation, "love your neighbors and hate your enemies" gets us: feuds such as the Hatfields and the McCoys; constant tensions such as in Northern Ireland, the Balkans, the Middle East, and elsewhere; racism in the United States and elsewhere; endless wars, each one supposed to end all wars. *How do we stop these cycles of decline and evil? How does God want us to stop them? Here, Jesus gives the answer. "Love your enemies; do good to those who hate you, etc. That's what it means to be an image of God."* What do you think and feel as you read what Jesus asks of us and these reflections? Perhaps you want to have a conversation with Jesus about these matters.

†

Where Are You in This Story?

With these teachings in the Sermon on the Mount, Jesus lays out for us what it means to live as members of the kingdom of God. And make no mistake about it. God wants us to live this way not just so that we can save ourselves but, even more important, so that we can help God to save the world. It's that simple and that stark.

But isn't it a wonderful ideal to aim for? Doesn't it stir you to want to join God in this great endeavor? Perhaps you don't react this way; your reaction may be fear or anger or a feeling of impotence to make any difference. Whatever your reactions, you can talk to Jesus or to God the Father about them. If you feel that what Jesus asks is beyond your capacity, you can tell him so and ask him for advice or for help to embrace his pointers and to try to implement them in your own life. Later in the book I will offer some examples of how people do live out these ways of following Jesus as a disciple.

How do you envision yourself in relation to Jesus right now? You have met him as the storyteller and teacher. Do his stories encourage you or give you pause? Do his teachings motivate you to take an active part in the greater story—or do they affect you in some other way?

7

Jesus Breaks the Hero Mold

Jesus clearly lived out his own teaching. During his public life he ate with tax collectors and sinners (Mark 2:4–17). Tax collectors were hated by the Jewish people not only because they worked for the Romans or for Herod Antipas but also because they enriched themselves through the taxes they collected. Sinners in Jewish tradition were people who openly flouted the law and seemed to care nothing for God. Moreover, Jesus ate with Pharisees, his strongest adversaries (Luke 7:36–50). But where he walked the walk most evidently was in Jerusalem during the last week of his short life on earth. Here he fulfilled the role of the suffering servant of Second Isaiah we discussed in chapter 5. It is to this suffering that we now turn, asking that we may know more intimately who God is and how God deals with evil.

The Suffering Servant

Crucifixions were relatively common in Jesus' time. The Roman occupiers used this punishment to sow fear in a populace and show who was boss. It seems that at some point in his public ministry Jesus realized that this was how he would die as Israel's Messiah. In what is likely the first Gospel written, Mark, Jesus first predicts his crucifixion after Peter has declared that he is the Messiah (Mark 8:27–31). This scene comes right after he has healed a blind man. Two more times before the end of chapter 10 he predicts his passion and death. After all three predictions, the disciples show by their behavior that they do not understand him. After the first, Peter tries to dissuade him, and Jesus calls him Satan (the tempter); after the second, the disciples argue on the road about who is the greatest; after the third, James and John ask Jesus if they can sit at his right and left in the kingdom, and the other ten become angry at them. Mark is showing that the apostles are like the blind men who bookended this section of the Gospel.

Let's not be too hard on the apostles. Remember that for them a crucified Messiah was a contradiction in terms. Someone who got crucified could not be the Messiah. Recall that the two who left the community of disciples for Emmaus on Easter morning said to the stranger they met on the road, "But we had hoped that he was the one who was going to redeem Israel" (Luke 24:21). Even though some of the women had found the tomb empty, these two left the community because, with Jesus dead by crucifixion, all was lost. He could not have been the Messiah. If we could put ourselves in their shoes, we, too, might be saying "We had hoped. . . ."

Jesus—the man with the great sense of humor and the great love for life and for people, the man who came to believe that he was the long-awaited Messiah of the Jewish people—now has concluded that being who he is will cost him his young life in a terrible way. *And that this is the way for God to win over evil: to let evil have its way with him and thus appear to triumph over him, and thus over God!* If he is the Messiah, there will be no other once he is crucified. It does bring home to us, doesn't it, how overwhelming it must have been for him to read the suffering servant songs of Isaiah now that he could see what they really meant for him?

We are accustomed to the hero of the story being the winner, the one left standing after the battle, the one who outwits those who try to destroy him. But Jesus is a different kind of hero, and his suffering brings a significant plot twist to the world's story.

You may want to spend some time with Mark's scenes of Jesus' predicting his passion and how he dealt with the obtuseness of his disciples. If so, then take some time with Mark 8:27—9:1; 9:30–37; and 10:32–45. If you do spend time with these scenes, ask Jesus to reveal to you his own feelings and his reactions to his apostles.

†

All four Gospels note that Jesus wanted to have a Passover meal before he died. Each Gospel has its own take on what happened at this meal. Mark, Matthew, and Luke (called the synoptic Gospels) recount that Jesus performed a special ritual with bread and a cup of wine, saying over the bread, "This is my body given up for you" and over the wine, "This is my blood of the covenant which is poured out for many." The Gospel of John does not have this ritual in its depiction of the Last Supper but does have long discourses by Jesus not mentioned in the other Gospels.

All the Gospel writers show Jesus as thinking more about his disciples—those at the meal and those who will follow—than about himself and what he will undergo the next day. The three synoptic Gospels note that Jesus predicted that Judas would hand him over to the Jewish authorities and that Peter would deny him, but Jesus wanted them to know how much he still loved them. And when he gave them the bread as his body and the wine as his blood, he told them to do this in remembrance of him. Clearly Jesus wanted them to continue to remember him and to stick together.

The Gospel of John dedicates four chapters, 13 to 17, to the Last Supper. In John's telling, Jesus spent a great deal of time trying to get the apostles ready for his crucifixion and to assure them of his continuing love for and presence to them afterward. In John, the supper opens with Jesus washing the feet of his apostles, an almost incredible act of generosity and love on this last night of his life on earth. And then he urges them to do the same for others. The leitmotif of being images of God keeps coming up, doesn't it? You may want to read prayerfully the scene of the washing in John 13:1–20 to get a sense of the atmosphere in the upper room at the beginning of John's description of the Last Supper. If you do this, imagine yourself in the scene, and see if you can let Jesus wash your feet.

I would like to spend some time now on John chapter 15. I suggest that you take some time to read that chapter prayerfully and then have a conversation with Jesus about his feelings at this time, and talk with him about your own reactions.

†

The image of the vine and branches is particularly powerful because of the unity between us and Jesus that the image proclaims. No branch can live for long unattached to the vine, can it? That's how close Jesus wants us to be to him in the kingdom that will begin with his death. In that kingdom, we will be asked to live as images of God; *this* we cannot do without him, for sure. This theme of unity will recur later in the supper when Jesus prays to the Father.

Right after he speaks of the vine and the branches, Jesus reminds his apostles (and us) of his desire that they love one another as he has loved them. Then he ups the ante.

> This is my commandment, that you love one another as I have loved you. No one has greater love than this, to lay down one's life for one's friends. You are my friends if you do what I command you. I do not call you servants any longer, because the servant does not know what the master is doing; but I have called you friends, because I have made known to you everything that I have heard from my Father. You did not choose me but I chose you. And I appointed you to go and bear fruit, fruit that will last, so that the Father will give you whatever you ask in

> my name. I am giving you these commands so that you may love one another. (John 15:12–17)

Jesus is telling them and us that we are his friends, for whom he will die a horrible death. And we are his friends, he says, because he has made known to us everything he has heard from the Father. Jesus has told us the most important things in his mind and heart, all that he knows of his Father. This is what we do with friends, isn't it, tell them what's most important to us, the deepest things in our hearts and minds? *And the thing that is most important to Jesus, because it's most important to his Father, is our loving one another. God has always wanted us humans to be the beloved community, a community that mirrors God's own triune self.*

What are your reactions and thoughts to my reflections on John 15? We are contemplating the mind and heart of Jesus on that night before he went to his death.

With chapter 17 we come to the climax of John's description of what happened at the Last Supper. Here Jesus directly addresses his beloved Father in an extraordinary prayer. We see what the Gospel writer believes was most on Jesus' mind and heart as he ended his festive meal with his friends. I suggest that you read the chapter prayerfully and spend some time reflecting on it and talking to Jesus about your reactions and his.

†

What always strikes me about this lovely prayer is that Jesus did not pray about what awaited him the next day; he prayed for the disciples eating with him, and later for all those who would come after them. Yes, he did ask the Father to glorify him, but even this was connected with others, those to whom he wanted to give eternal life. In John's Gospel, Jesus is glorified precisely on the cross. Jesus here demonstrates the love for his friends that he spoke of earlier.

Notice the definition of "eternal life": to know the Father and Jesus, the Messiah (Christ), whom he has sent. Eternal life comes down to knowing and loving God. "Knowing" in the Bible does not refer to head knowledge only; it means heart knowledge, the kind of knowledge friends and lovers have of one another. It's the kind of knowledge that comes from spending time with the other rather than from reading about or studying the other. If you will, it's the kind of knowledge of God you have been gaining through the prayerful reflection on the Bible during the reading of this book.

In the next section of the prayer (vv. 6–19), Jesus speaks to his Father about these apostles at table with him. He reminds his Father that these men are just as much the Father's as Jesus' friends. "All mine are yours, and yours are mine" (v. 10). "Holy Father, protect them in your name that you have given me, so that they may be one, as we are one" (v. 11). Jesus, it seems, is almost obsessed with their need for unity with one another. And the reason is that they are images of God, who is a unity of three in a profoundly mysterious way. *I have been pondering this unity for a long time, and I have come to the conclusion that from the beginning of time God has wanted human beings to reflect God's own triune unity in this world. Jesus' prayer reflects that great mystery and God's deepest desire in creating us.* How do you react to his reflection? Does it make sense to you?

The rest of this section of the prayer reflects Jesus' concern for the future of his friends. He begs the Father to protect them, to keep them safe from the evil one and from "the world." Let me say something about what "the world" means here. It can sound as though Jesus (and his Father) disdain the world. But remember that God is the creator of the world and that world is declared "good" in the first chapter of Genesis. The book of Wisdom puts it strongly:

> For you love all things that exist,
> and detest none of the things that you have made,

> for you would not have made anything if you had
> hated it.
> (Wisdom 11:24).

And in John 3:16, the author of the Gospel writes, "For God so loved the world that he gave his only Son, so that everyone who believes in him may not perish but may have eternal life." When the Gospel speaks of "the world" in a pejorative way, it is referring to the world as alienated from God; that world is a danger to Jesus' friends. *In the terms I have been using in this book, we could say that the world as a danger is the world under the sway of Satan, the world of the downward cycle of decline from God's dream.*

In the next to last section (John 17:20–24) Jesus prays for all those "who will believe in me through their word." He is praying for us as well as all those throughout the ages who have come to believe in him. Notice, again, that unity is at the heart of what he prays for, and the unity is profound: "that they may all be one. As you, Father, are in me and I am in you, may they also be in us, so that the world may believe that you have sent me" (vv. 20–21).

He repeats the same prayer again. "The glory that you have given me I have given them, so that they may be one, as we are one, I in them and you in me, that they may become completely one, so that the world may know that you have sent me and have loved them even as you have loved me" (John 17:22–23). Jesus prays that our unity with others mirrors the unity of the Holy Trinity.

Here Jesus underlines again that the unity of Jesus' friends is what will convince the world of the truth about Jesus. In fact, there is some evidence that it was precisely this love that did draw people to Christianity in the early centuries. "See how they love one another" was said by outsiders. And they also loved their non-Christian neighbors as well. "Are we as attractive in our day?" might be a good question to ask ourselves.

As the prayer develops, Jesus seems to get more and more insistent on the unity he and the Father desire among us, a unity that mirrors the unity of Father, Son, and Holy Spirit. "Mirrors" may not actually be a strong enough word for what Jesus and the Father want; Jesus seems to want us to be united with him and the Father by the same love that unites him with the Father. Does that flabbergast you? It often does me. One way to grasp what Jesus prays for here is to think that he is probably speaking of the Holy Spirit who, in a sense, is the love that unites Father and Son and whom Jesus promised to send upon his disciples at this Last Supper. It's beyond comprehension. But then again God is beyond comprehension. We don't have to understand it; we just need to live out in our lives as best we can the unity God offers us. So perhaps Jesus is just trying with human words to hint at the actual mystery of the union God wants with us and among us.

The final words of this prayer touch on this profound mystery, don't they? "So that the love with which you have loved me may be in them, and I in them" (John 17:26). Let these words sink in. I hope that you realize how much you, and all of us, are loved by Jesus and his Father.

The Story's Bleakest Moments

Now we come to the awful ending of Jesus' life. By undergoing crucifixion, he becomes the suffering servant of Second Isaiah. Jesus takes on the suffering that was the consequence of the cycles of evil to which all of us have contributed, and he does it in such a way that the cycle of evil is definitively defeated.

I suggest that you read prayerfully the account of the Passion in Luke's Gospel. You will find it in Luke 22:47—23:56. Take your time; read it carefully, pausing often to talk to Jesus, if so moved.

†

It's a terribly sad story, isn't it? How did you react to Judas's kiss? It must have broken Jesus' heart. You must have noticed how Jesus' jailers treated him with contempt, ridicule, and violence. As often happens when someone is condemned to death, these jailers treat Jesus as less than human. Jesus has become expendable, as have so many people throughout human history.

But we remember that Jesus was the Messiah, the actual Son of God, and he was treated as though he did not matter much at all. We must also remember that Jesus himself said that what we do, for good or ill, to anyone, we do to him (Matthew 25).

In Luke's Passion narrative, one of Jesus' followers drew a sword and cut off the ear of the high priest's slave. Jesus's response was "No more of this," after which he healed the slave's ear (Luke 22:49–51). Then he freely gave himself up but not without speaking the truth to power: "Have you come out with swords and clubs as if I were a bandit? When I was with you day after day in the temple, you did not lay hands on me. But this is your hour, and the power of darkness!" (Luke 22:52–53). Jesus may have surrendered, but he did not stop telling his captors the truth. This is how God meets evil: not with a gun, but with truth and love.

I felt compassion for Peter when he came under the questioning of the servant girl and others. Most likely I would have acted no differently. At that moment, fear had him by the throat, and so he denied his beloved friend and master. As you contemplated his denial and Jesus looking at him, what did you see in Jesus' eyes? I imagined that the look was sad and, at the same time, caring. I felt that Peter's denials must have hurt Jesus badly, but they did not extinguish his love for Peter. Haven't you been angered by a friend's betrayal and, at the same time, felt care and love for your friend? I have been the recipient of both these reactions from a friend I hurt, as, no doubt, you have been. Perhaps, human beings at our best act in this way because we are created as images of God who acts this way all the time.

Whenever I read the section where the leaders of Jesus' religion question him and then decide, with almost mob-like vehemence, to condemn him, I feel both anger and sadness, anger that they are so bent on getting this innocent man killed, sadness that they turn away from the very Messiah whom they and their fellow Jews have for centuries dreamt of. I also feel some compassion for Jesus and for God the Father who so love their Chosen People.

And I think of how often in the history of the Christian church, leaders have acted completely contrary to the way of

Jesus. Just think of the way, over centuries, Christian leaders treated Jews in many parts of Europe, forcing them to live in ghettoes where they were constantly in danger of attack. Or think of the period of the Inquisition in many European countries when so many innocent people were convicted by religious courts of being heretics and were condemned to torturous deaths. We can think of many other cases of behavior by Christians that were completely at odds with the teachings of Jesus. In Jesus, God suffered these cruelties and, remarkably, still kept loving those who did the deeds. It's enough to make you feel compassion and love for God, isn't it?

The scene with Herod is sickening. He treats Jesus as a trickster or a buffoon, someone sent for his and his court's entertainment. No wonder Jesus refuses to say a word here. I paused here, realizing that these sentences were filled with contempt for Herod and his minions. I said to myself, "Is that the way Jesus' silence should be interpreted? Was he contemptuous?" Perhaps my pause and question were prompted by the Spirit of Jesus. I find it hard to think that Jesus was ever contemptuous of anyone. But I did write the first three sentences of this paragraph. It's an example, I believe, of how much my reactions are influenced by a spirit that is not the Spirit of Jesus. We are, after all, creatures of a culture that clearly is not suffused with the Spirit of Jesus. I doubt that Jesus' silence signaled contempt; I am now more inclined to see it as a sign of his anger at the decadence of Herod's court and sadness that images of God could have sunk this low. What comes to mind as you imagine this scene with Herod?

†

In Pilate, Jesus confronts a vacillating Roman procurator of Judea who, for whatever reason, seems to want to do the right thing. But he fears a riot more than he fears doing the wrong thing. In a way, Pilate was moved by the same logic as the high priest Caiaphas, who said, "You do not understand that it is better for you to have one man die for the people than to have the whole nation destroyed" (John 11:50). For Pilate, the death of this innocent Jew, it seems, was the only way to stop a riot. Both men were willing to kill one innocent man to save themselves and, perhaps, their jobs. However, neither Caiaphas nor Pilate realized that God has a plan to overcome evil by this terrible death. As the Gospel of John notes, without knowing it, Caiaphas, as high priest that year, was prophesying for God. God's ways, indeed, are not our ways.

The shouts of the crowd, demanding the crucifixion of Jesus, are searing, aren't they? Jesus was the Messiah the Jewish people had looked forward to all their lives. Now he was in front of them, and they shouted "Crucify, crucify him!" They went so far as to ask for the release of a known criminal, Barabbas, instead of Jesus. The terrible irony is that Jesus' crucifixion will bring about God's victory, the onset of the kingdom of God, the same kingdom to which the Israelites were called as God's people centuries ago. Now they were caught up in hatred and the desire for blood that can take control of a crowd. Satan was having a field day in his hatred of God. It looked as though the cycle of evil would finally win. But God had other plans, plans motivated by love; Satan met his match in Jesus of Nazareth.

Jesus faced evil in the religious leaders, in Pilate, in Herod, and in Peter just as he had done all his public life. The cycles of decline were present all the time, but so were the cycles of love moving out from Jesus. Our faith in God tells us that the latter will prevail because their source is God who is love.

It's important to point out that both Jews and Gentiles joined forces to destroy Jesus. The implication is that all of us are stained by this awful act. But God's love, shown in Jesus' willingness to accept the worst that hate can do and not respond in kind, wants to transform the evil we do by facing it with love.

On his way to Calvary, Jesus met a group of Jewish women weeping over what was happening to him. In his remarks to them he showed his compassion for them and for his people, another instance of how he thought of others even in this dark hour.

I'm sure you noticed what Jesus said at Calvary: "Father, forgive them; for they do not know what they are doing" (Luke 23:34). Here we see how love meets evil. We see almost immediately how Jesus' words and whole approach to his crucifixion affected one of the criminals beside him. He rebuked his fellow criminal and spoke warmly to Jesus: "Jesus, remember me when you come into your kingdom" (23:42). Love, it seems, has transformed this man.

Finally, after nine hours of agony on the cross, Jesus speaks his last words: "Father, into your hands I commend my spirit" and breathes his last (Luke 23:46). The agony is over. Out of love for us, the suffering servant has taken on the suffering and death all of us deserve. Let's recall part of the fourth servant song now:

> Surely he has borne our infirmities
> and carried our diseases;
> yet we accounted him stricken,

struck down by God, and afflicted.
But he was wounded for our transgressions,
crushed for our iniquities;
upon him was the punishment that made us whole,
and by his bruises we are healed.
All we like sheep have gone astray;
we have all turned to our own way,
and the LORD has laid on him
the iniquity of us all.
He was oppressed and he was afflicted,
yet he did not open his mouth;
like a lamb that is led to slaughter,
and like a sheep that before his shearers is silent,
so he did not open his mouth.
(Isaiah 53:4–7)

As I was typing the part of the song above, one line—"upon him was the punishment that made us whole"—struck me deeply. Because he accepted this suffering, we are made whole. I feel a great burst of gratitude for what Jesus did for us on Good Friday.

I'm sure that if I were one of his disciples at the time, I, too, would have cut and run. In fear I might well have denied knowing Jesus, as did Peter. All of us, as Paul writes, "have sinned and fall short of the glory of God" (Romans 3:23). But in some mysterious way, Jesus' death on the cross has saved us from our weakness, folly, and sinfulness. Jesus looked into the face of evil and did not flinch; he continued to love even those who were driving the nails into his hands and feet, even those who taunted him as he died. He was God in human flesh and in that human flesh faced down evil with love, thus starting a great cycle of love that still moves through our world as more and more of us humans follow him and act as the images of God we are created to be.

Jesus' love may well have touched the heart of the centurion who led the Roman soldiers who crucified Jesus. Luke writes, "When the centurion saw what had taken place, he praised God and said, 'Certainly this man was innocent'" (Luke 23:47). In Mark's version the centurion says, "Truly this man was God's Son!" Perhaps this event was a great turning point in the centurion's life and led to his doing more good than harm from then on. We can hope.

Where Are You in This Story?

In W. H. Vanstone's *The Stature of Waiting*, he does a careful analysis of the Gospels to show that in his public life Jesus is characterized as being an active participant in what happens to him and around him, but that in his Passion he is a passive recipient of what others do to him. He spends a whole chapter, for example, showing, from an analysis of the Greek of the Gospels, that in all but one case Judas is said to "hand Jesus over" rather than to "betray him." Those words *handing over* seem to have been the way the Gospel writers described what was happening to Jesus throughout the Passion. Once Jesus was "handed over," he became a person who waited on others to know what would happen to him.

Vanstone believes that Jesus had determined to force a choice on the Jewish leaders about who he was. His entry into Jerusalem on a donkey with crowds of Galilean peasants coming to Jerusalem for Passover was chosen to show to these leaders that he did have sizeable support for his claims to be the Messiah. Vanstone argues that he knew that the Jewish leaders would not pay attention to him if he was a lone individual. He also knew that this was a risky venture; in fact, he seems to have presumed that it would lead to his death. But he had to put the choice clearly before them, accepting him as the Messiah—along with his way of being Messiah—or rejecting him.

Vanstone's version makes sense to me. Eventually, the Messiah had to be accepted by the Jewish people for them to fulfill the deepest purpose of being the Chosen People of God. By entering Jerusalem in the way he did, Jesus was putting the choice before the leadership. These last days in

Jerusalem were Jesus' final actions to try to convince the leaders of who he was.

After the supper with his disciples, Jesus, therefore, went to the Garden of Gethsemane to await the choice of the leaders. He was now waiting, not acting. The next step was up to others, not him. Hence, in a sense, by what he did in entering Jerusalem and then dispersing the money changers in the temple, he handed himself over to others to decide his fate. Would they believe him or not?

I read Vanstone's book as I was nearing the end of this chapter. It struck me as a confirmation of what I had been writing to this point. From the very beginning of creation, God has been acting as Jesus acted during his life and, especially, as he neared its end. By creating us for friendship and cooperation with God in his dream for our world, God has been both active in continual creation and in trying to draw us into living as people made in God's image. At the same time, God has been waiting for our response. We might say that from the beginning of our universe God has been both active and passive, passive in the sense that God waits for our acceptance of the offer of friendship with all that such friendship entails. It's a great mystery indeed. How can God who is impassible—unconstrained by anyone or anything outside Godself—be passive? God is mystery. We can never comprehend who God is or what God can do. But the reality seems to be that God has freely put himself into a waiting pose before us by creating us humans who have free will. Vanstone puts the matter this way:

> It can be no coincidence that the writer who in his Gospel most clearly discerns the glory of God in the handing over of Jesus is also the writer who, in the first of his Epistles, makes the memorable declaration that "God is love." For love, as it is known imperfectly and fragmentarily in human experience, is precisely the "shape" which John discerns in the life of Jesus. Love acts of its own initiative, under no compulsion or constraint, in order that another may benefit; and the activity which is characteristic of love is, in principle, without limit or qualification. In loving one offers no limited proportion of what one has and is; one expends, or at least makes available, the whole of one's resources. But this unlimited expenditure is made for the sake of an other—in order that an other may receive; and, whenever that other is no mere extension of oneself but truly an other, then it must remain in doubt whether that other will in fact receive. In authentic loving there is no control of the other who is loved; that he or she will receive is beyond the power of love to ordain or know.[2]

Do you see what this means? Jesus has, in a sense, proven that he is God's Son by handing himself over to the Jewish leaders in love. Then he waits as God waits throughout history for the response. Will they accept this love or not? If these leaders do accept this love, i.e., accept who God is, then they will have to change their lives, i.e., undergo a conversion of mind and heart. Then they will have been transformed from their destructive ways of living to God's way of being human, and the transformation will not be by force, but by love.

Vanstone continues, "The most glorious activity of God is that He hands Himself over, and, in His free activity of loving, surrenders His own impassibility."[3] By choosing to love us humans and to become human, God has shown that vulnerability is in a mysterious way a trait of God. It is difficult to understand, for sure, but it is a conclusion almost forced on us by the revelation that God is love.

How do you feel after accompanying Jesus through this story's bleakest moments, when all seemed lost? How do you respond to the way he acted in the midst of everything seeming to fall apart? What can you say to him about the bleak moments you may face now and the terrors and death the world faces in this time?

8

The Plot Takes a Huge Twist

As we begin this chapter, let's ask to be able to enter prayerfully the minds and hearts of the disciples after the death of Jesus. With that request made, I suggest reading the next couple of paragraphs based on Luke's account of the Resurrection appearances.

Imagine how devastated they were at the end of that awful Friday. It's perhaps a measure of their love for Jesus, and the glimmer of hope some of his words about resurrection gave them, that most of them seemed to stay together. The men must have been rather sheepish, perhaps even deeply guilty, knowing that they all had abandoned Jesus. But all of them, men and women, must have been heartbroken and wondered whether they had backed the wrong messiah. Still, something kept them together over the Saturday Sabbath and into Sunday.

Jesus' Resurrection

On Sunday morning, when the women went to the tomb to anoint Jesus' body, they found the stone moved and the tomb empty. According to Luke, they saw two men in dazzling robes who told them that Jesus was risen and reminded them of what Jesus had told them in Galilee, that after he was crucified he would rise on the third day. When the women returned to the disciples and told them what had happened, they took the news as an idle tale. Peter did go to the tomb and found it empty as the women had said, but they were all still unconvinced.

That's when two of them left the group and headed to Emmaus, perhaps so disheartened that they couldn't stand being with the rest anymore. You will remember their despairing words: "We had hoped . . ." from the last chapter. When they returned joyfully to the group, they found that Jesus had appeared to Peter and the mood had changed dramatically. It must have lifted even more when these two told their story of meeting Jesus and recognizing him in the breaking of the bread.

I hope that you have felt some of their despair and the gloom that must have prevailed. Feeling that, you may feel more deeply their astonished joy at what has happened. Then Luke presents the following scene.

> While they were talking about this, Jesus himself stood among them and said to them, "Peace be with you." They were startled and terrified, and thought that they were seeing a ghost. He said to them, "Why are you frightened, and why do doubts arise in your hearts? Look at my hands and my feet; see that it is I myself. Touch me and see, for a ghost does not have flesh and bones as you see that I have." And when he had said this, he showed them his hands and his feet. While in their joy they were disbelieving and still wondering, he said to them, "Have you anything here to eat?" They gave him a piece of broiled fish, and he took it and ate in their presence. (Luke 24:36–43)

How did you feel as you prayerfully read about this appearance? Maybe you would like to talk with Jesus about his reactions and your own.

The appearances of Jesus were all surprising; Jesus seemed to come out of nowhere and to disappear rather quickly. I can understand why the disciples were startled, perhaps terrified, and had a hard time recognizing him and believing their own eyes and ears. But here, as in other appearances, Jesus did something that only someone with a body could do. On this evening, he asked for something to eat and then ate the fish. He also ate fish when he appeared at the lake in John 21. In what was possibly an inn on the road to Emmaus, he had a meal with the two disciples, and they recognized him in the breaking of the bread. In John's Gospel, Mary Magdalene finally recognized him when he said her name. You can understand the difficulties the disciples had. Jesus had died and was buried. They did not expect to see him again. But now he was here. It must have been bewildering.

But the texts also mention great joy. Perhaps they experienced how joyful Jesus was and it rubbed off on them even before it fully dawned on them that he was truly alive. Recently in prayer, I was contemplating one of these Resurrection scenes. I imagined being there and asked Jesus about his joy. What came to me was that he, too, being human, had to go into his Passion with faith that God would save the world this way. If this is so, then the joy he felt when raised from the dead would have been overpowering indeed.

No matter how wise or learned we are, faith is not sight. Faith means trusting that God exists and that God actually is the creator of our universe. With that trust a believer bets everything that it's true. I'm only going on my own experience and that of others who have entrusted their experience to me. When we, by God's grace, see God face-to-face, we will then know with certainty that what we believed was and is true. I can imagine how wildly joyful that blessed event would be. No more questions and fears. Just immense relief and wild joy, I imagine. What do you think?

I admit that I don't know how faith worked for the Word made flesh; no one in this life ever did or does. In imagining Jesus' life experiences, we are left with our own experience. If, however, I am more on target than off, then the joy Jesus exuded when he appeared to his mother and to the disciples must have been off the charts. What are your reactions and thoughts? Does it ring true to you? Maybe you have something to talk over with Jesus at this time. Go ahead, the rest of the book will still be there when you finish.

Jesus' joy must have almost overwhelmed the disciples. Luke writes, "While in their joy they were disbelieving" (24:41). Luke is trying to describe that mix of joy and disbelief that comes to us when something totally unexpected and very joyful happens. Think of a mother who believes her son has died in a car crash only to find out that the son is still alive and will recuperate. She can't believe it because she wanted it to be true though it seemed impossible. Does that make sense to you?

The other thing I notice in all the appearances is that Jesus does not say a word of reprimand to the disciples who had denied and abandoned him. Not one word. The only appearance that might give this impression is in John 21, when Jesus asked Peter three times, "Do you love me?" But I have never heard or read of anyone interpreting these questions as a way for Jesus to reprimand Peter for his denials. Rather, it is taken that Jesus, in this kind way, let Peter know that his threefold denial was not the end of him as a disciple. Jesus told him, "Feed my sheep," thus assuring him that Jesus still wanted him as a friend and collaborator.

Earlier in the Gospel we heard, "For God so loved the world that he gave his only Son, so that everyone who believes in him may not perish but may have eternal life. Indeed, God did not send the Son into the world to condemn the world, but in order that the world might be saved through him" (John 3:16–17). In these appearances Jesus demonstrated the truth of that saying; he did not condemn or even reprimand, but continued to love those who had abandoned and denied him, and even those who had put him to death.

What do you think? How do you react? Do you want to say anything to Jesus or ask him anything? Go ahead.

†

Enter the Holy Spirit

At the Last Supper, Jesus had promised to send his Spirit as an advocate and helper to his disciples. In John's Gospel the sending of the Spirit occurs on Easter Sunday evening when Jesus appears in the upper room although the doors were locked. In chapter 20 the writer notes, at the beginning and now here, that it was the first day of the week, indicating that this was the beginning of the new creation, the promised kingdom of God. Remember that in Genesis 1 creation began on the first day of the week. Let's read prayerfully what happened at this appearance.

> Jesus came and stood among them and said, "Peace be with you." After he said this, he showed them his hands and his side. Then the disciples rejoiced when they saw the Lord. Jesus said to them again, "Peace be with you. As the Father has sent me, so I send you." When he said this, he breathed on them and said to them, "Receive the Holy Spirit. If you forgive the sins of any, they are forgiven them; if you retain the sins of any, they are retained." (John 20:19–23)

John's Gospel opened with "In the beginning was the Word," reminding readers of the first creation. At that first creation the Spirit, translated as "wind" in the NRSV, "swept over the face of the waters" (Genesis 1:2). (In both

Hebrew and Greek, the same word can be translated as "spirit," "breath," or "wind.") So now, at this new creation, the Spirit comes upon the disciples as Jesus *breathed* on them. The coming of the Messiah, in Jewish lore, would be accompanied by the forgiveness of sins. This, I think, is the significance of Jesus giving the disciples the power to forgive sins.

This story does not tell us of the effects on the disciples of this outpouring of the Spirit. But we do know from the Acts of the Apostles and the other books of the New Testament that the disciples, who locked the doors because of fear, boldly preached after this.

Before we move on to the scene of the outpouring of the Spirit in the Acts of the Apostles, let's take some time to relish what we have just read. How are you affected by this story? Perhaps you feel moved to talk with Jesus about his joy and the joy he seems so eager to impart to his friends, including you.

The Birth of the Beloved Community

In the Acts of the Apostles, the sending of the Spirit occurs on the Jewish feast of Pentecost, also called the Feast of

Weeks. That feast occurred seven weeks after Passover, fifty days after Jesus' death. Sometime before this particular Pentecost, the risen Jesus had left his disciples, having promised to send the Spirit. Let's read the text in Acts prayerfully and then reflect on our reactions.

> When the day of Pentecost had come, they were all together in one place. And suddenly from heaven there came a sound like the rush of a violent wind, and it filled the entire house where they were sitting. Divided tongues, as of fire, appeared among them, and a tongue rested on each of them. All of them were filled with the Holy Spirit and began to speak in other languages, as the Spirit gave them ability. (Acts 2:1–4)

Remember that in Hebrew and Greek, the same word is translated "spirit," "wind," or "breath." The "sound like the rush of a violent wind" signifies the presence of the Spirit of God in a special way. Perhaps you will experience the wind differently now that you associate it so intimately with the Spirit of God.

As did the scene in the upper room in John, the scene in Acts also harks back to Genesis but in this case to chapter 11 and the Tower of Babel. Acts is indicating that the inability to understand one another because of our different languages is now overcome by the gift of the Spirit. In the next section of this scene, we read that the apostles began to preach and were understood by people of different languages who had come to Jerusalem for the festival. This is another story indicating that, with Jesus' life, death, and resurrection, we have entered a new creation. Cycles of sin and decline are being transformed into cycles of love and development by the love of God poured out into the hearts of human beings by the gift of the Holy Spirit.

Remember how fearful these disciples were after Jesus' crucifixion. Now they speak boldly and openly of Jesus to their Jewish brothers and sisters. Peter himself gives a long speech, apparently on this very day. If you have not read that speech in some time, you might want to do so now in Acts 2:14–37.

†

This is a remarkable speech by a man who only seven weeks earlier denied he knew Jesus and who cowered in the upper room after Jesus died. The gift of the Spirit has transformed him. Notice that he does not mince words; to this Jewish audience he speaks of Jesus of Nazareth, whom "you crucified and killed by the hands of those outside the law" (Acts 2:23). "Those outside the law" are, of course, the Romans. Despite the fact that many of them may have asked for

Jesus' crucifixion, they are now invited to repent and be baptized in Jesus' name. God is love indeed.

After the speech, Peter reminds them that "the promise is for you" (Acts 2:39). Even though they had killed the Messiah, God still remains true to his promise to and covenant with the Chosen People. That's amazing, isn't it? Peter, it seems, has grasped how God's love transforms sinners and creates cycles of love and peace where before there were cycles of decline, discord, and hate. Peter himself has felt that transformation in himself and preaches it to the very people who killed Jesus.

Three thousand in the crowd are transformed by Peter's speech. "Now when they heard this, they were cut to the heart and said to Peter and to the other apostles, 'Brothers, what should we do?'" (Acts 2:37). Peter told them to repent and be baptized. "So those who welcomed his message were baptized, and that day about three thousand persons were added. They devoted themselves to the apostles' teaching and fellowship, to the breaking of bread and the prayers" (2:41–42). Peter's preaching could have set off a riot and killing, but because he spoke with love and honesty, they were won over and began a new way of life. These three thousand joined the cycle of good introduced into the world by the coming of the Spirit.

Two chapters later, Acts describes the life of the first Christian community in Jerusalem.

> "Now the whole group of those who believed were of one heart and soul, and no one claimed private ownership of any possessions, but everything they owned was held in common. With great power the apostles gave their testimony to the resurrection of the Lord Jesus, and great grace was upon them all. There was not a needy person among them, for as many as owned lands or houses sold them and brought the proceeds of what was sold. They laid it at the apostles' feet, and it was distributed to each as any had need." (Acts 4:32–35)

These early disciples seem to have become the Beloved Community that God has wanted among us since the foundation of the world. The description may be idealized, but it does get at the dream God has for us and indicates that the early community of believers in Jesus tried to live out the kingdom of God here on earth. No doubt the reality was messier than is depicted here, but they seem to have tried to live as Jesus wanted them to live, and with remarkable effects.

Sit with your response to this story of the Pentecost. What goes through your mind? How do feel about what you have read? Can you bring any of this to Jesus in prayer?

†

The small remnant after Jesus' death seems to have grown rapidly in the city where he was killed. These Jewish converts to Jesus' way were considered a danger by the leaders of Judaism. Beginning in chapter 5 of Acts we find these leaders threatening, jailing, and flogging the apostles, trying to make them keep quiet about Jesus. But the apostles would not remain quiet. Persecutions broke out, Stephen was stoned to death, and in chapter 8 we read,

> That day a severe persecution began against the church in Jerusalem, and all except the apostles were scattered throughout the countryside of Judea and Samaria. Devout men buried Stephen and made loud lamentation over him. But Saul was ravaging the church by entering house after house; dragging off both men and women, he committed them to prison. (Acts 8:1–3)

It seems that whenever people take God seriously and begin to act as images of God, hackles rise, not just in the secular realm but also among people of religion. Just look at First Kings and see how the prophet Elijah was treated by King Ahab, his wife Jezebel, and some of the people of Israel when he worked to restore worship of the true God. Or see how the prophet Jeremiah was treated by the inhabitants of Jerusalem when he spoke the warnings of Yahweh. If we do act as people made in God's image, we must not expect that everyone will approve of us. Ignatius of Loyola warned Jesuits to examine their minds and hearts if they were too much admired because it could mean that they were not speaking truly of God. People who do speak and act in God's way will never be easily accepted by those who rule this world, nor by many who profit from the way the world now runs.

The scattering of the community led to the expansion of believers in Jesus and to more persecutions. Saul was one of those who persecuted followers of Jesus. In Acts chapter 9 we find Saul asking the high priest for letters to the synagogues at Damascus. He intended to go there with a cohort to find believers in Jesus and bring them, bound, back to Jerusalem to be tried. On his fateful journey, we read,

> Suddenly a light from heaven flashed around him. He fell to ground and heard a voice saying to him, "Saul, Saul, why do you persecute me?" He asked, "Who are you, Lord?" The reply came, "I am Jesus, whom you are persecuting. But get up and enter the city, and you will be told what you are to do." The men who were traveling with him stood speechless because they heard the voice but saw no one. Saul got up from the ground, and though his eyes were open, he could see nothing; so they led him by the hand and brought him into Damascus.

> For three days he was without sight, and neither ate nor drank. (Acts 9:3–9)

In Damascus, Saul was visited by Ananias, a follower of Jesus who had been told in a vision that he should lay hands on Saul to restore his sight. Ananias knew of Saul's persecutions of Christians and was rightfully taken aback. "But the Lord said to him, 'Go, for he is an instrument whom I have chosen to bring my name before Gentiles and kings and before the people of Israel'" (Acts 9:15). Through Ananias, Saul received his sight back and was baptized. Here again we see how God works to overcome evil. Saul was not killed or shunted aside; rather, he was taken into the fellowship of those he had just been persecuting and, given his talents, was offered a mission to foster the growth of that fellowship. God does not destroy but transforms.

Pause for a while with this story of Paul. What are your reactions? What is your prayer?

Everything Is Possible

Most of the rest of Acts is taken up with the mission to the Gentiles. In these early days, the followers of Jesus remained attached to the temple in Jerusalem. They considered themselves faithful Jews who believed that Jesus was the long-awaited Messiah, who would come again at the end of time to bring to completion the kingdom of God. With the scattering of many of them that we just read about, more followers of Jesus ended up in neighboring countries. Gentiles began to show interest, and the question this raised was whether they had to convert to Judaism to be baptized. One significant incident that helped settle this difficult issue happened to Peter. This is recounted in chapter 10 of Acts. I suggest that you read this chapter prayerfully and then have a conversation with God about your thoughts and reactions.

Please note that Simon/Peter was still an orthodox Jew. In the vision he refused to eat unclean creatures, and when he entered the house of Cornelius, he told him, "You yourselves know that it is unlawful for a Jew to associate with or visit a Gentile" (Acts 10:28). But the vision had shaken up his understanding of the law: "What God has made clean, you must not call profane" (Acts 10:15). Because of his vision, Peter was prepared to follow Cornelius's servants. He had become at least this open.

Americans who are old enough remember that in parts of this country strict segregation of the races was the law. African Americans had to sit separately on buses and trains, use separate toilet facilities, and eat separately from white

Americans. Even as I write, the racism that led to such indignities still plagues the lives of African Americans. We might want to talk to God about these matters as we ponder the difficulties of the earliest Jewish Christians in overcoming their own strong and deep-seated prejudice.

When Peter entered Cornelius's house, he was still not sure what he was supposed to do. "Now may I ask why you sent for me" (Acts 10:29). Cornelius then told Peter what had happened to him as he was praying and ended with, "Now all of us are here in the presence of God to listen to all that the Lord has commanded you to say" (10:33). Peter responded generously, "I truly understand that God shows no partiality, but in every nation anyone who fears him and does what is right is acceptable to him" (10:34–35) and went on to explain about Jesus and his mission.

For Peter, the final proof of what he should do came before he even finished speaking, when "the Holy Spirit fell upon all who heard the word" (Acts 10:44) stunning the men who came with Peter. Peter then ordered that all the Gentiles be baptized in the name of Jesus Christ, and to top it off, Peter and his companions stayed with Cornelius for several days.

You will have noticed that Peter and his companions were not persuaded by arguments but by the facts before their eyes and ears. Later, when Peter had to defend his actions with the apostles and others in Judea who were outraged by what he'd done, he just told them what happened, step-by-step, and they were mollified. "When they heard this, they were silenced. And they praised God, saying, 'Then God has given even to the Gentiles the repentance that leads to life'" (Acts 11:18).

The issue of how to deal with Gentiles was not settled with Peter's experience. It proved a very tough nut to crack for the Jewish Christians. It could have destroyed the Jesus movement, or at least profoundly impeded its forward movement, if it had been handled differently, or if Peter and the rest of that early band had not paid attention to the promptings of the Spirit within and around them. The problems did not end with Peter's change of heart or with Saul's conversion, as we will see.

The movement forward continued through paying attention to the promptings of the Holy Spirit, and those promptings always move toward love and more and more inclusion. The evil of disunion among human beings is being overcome by the transforming of hearts and minds. But the unity that was and continues to be developed (the Beloved Community, if you will) is always in danger because all human hearts are also influenced by counter-movements that lead to disunity. No wonder Jesus was so concerned about unity at the Last Supper as detailed in John's Gospel.

Now, back to Saul, who has become Paul. He and Barnabas were missioned by the Christians at Antioch to spread the message of Jesus around the Mediterranean world, first in Asia Minor and then into Europe through Greece. When Paul entered a new town or city, he seems to have first approached the Jews of the area, but when he was often maltreated by those Jews who were not convinced by his arguments, he turned to the Gentiles. The movement grew steadily through his preaching and that of others.

As more and more Gentiles entered the communities founded by Paul, they were not required to accept all the Jewish customs, one of which was the circumcision of males. Tensions simmered, especially within the community in Jerusalem. Some of these believers came to Antioch and "were teaching the brothers, 'Unless you are circumcised according to the custom of Moses, you cannot be saved'" (Acts 15:1). Paul and Barnabas had strong arguments with these men, as a result of which Paul and Barnabas and others were sent to Jerusalem "to discuss this question with the apostles and the elders" (15:2).

At this point I suggest that you read prayerfully what took place in Jerusalem to settle this matter. The text is in Acts 15:6–35. As you read it, pay attention to your own reactions and thoughts. They may give you something to discuss with the Lord.

†

What is most remarkable in this telling of their proceedings is the way they seem to have handled the issues. I'm sure that they had some hot arguments, especially in the beginning, as the members who had been Pharisees said that the Gentile converts needed to be circumcised. But in this telling, the tone is different. They listened to one another tell stories of how the Spirit had worked among the Gentiles. Peter started it off by telling his story and making his pitch that they should not make the Gentiles do something they themselves have found burdensome. Then Paul and Barnabas had their say.

Finally, James, the brother of Jesus, who seems to have had a leadership position in the Jerusalem community, made his position clear based on what he had heard. He cited Peter's testimony and then the prophets Amos and Isaiah who spoke of how the Gentiles would worship the one true God. He followed up with the tender words,

"Therefore I have reached the decision that we should not trouble those Gentiles who are turning to God" (Acts 15:19). With this statement James seems to have moved the whole assembly to a unanimous agreement to write that warm, generous, and straightforward letter to the church at Antioch that ends the council of Jerusalem.

What wins out here is love: love for Jesus, love for one another, and love for the Gentiles who were their new sisters and brothers. When we recall that some of this group were members of the "sect of the Pharisees," the group who had been most opposed to Jesus during his life, then we realize that the Holy Spirit has enabled a remarkable transformation in some of this group. Love has made enemies into friends. A cycle of good has entered our world with far-reaching consequences over time. If this council had come up with a different solution, say, requiring that all male converts be circumcised, the Jesus movement would have gone on in a much different direction, which would have had an entirely different impact on our grand story.

This last point is quite important. How we act does have consequences, not just for ourselves but also for others in our world. We do not know the long-term consequences of our acts, but they are real. In my own case, I remind you of the effects on me of a question a Xaverian brother asked me when I was nearing graduation from high school, as I mentioned in the Prologue. He asked what I was going to do after high school. When I answered, truthfully, "I don't know," he said, "Why don't you go to college?" That suggestion pushed me to apply to the College of the Holy Cross in Worcester, which put me in contact with the Jesuits. Thus, that question changed my life, but also, I believe, changed the lives of many others whom I have met and/or served over the past seventy years as a Jesuit. It may even be affecting you now.

I want to end this chapter with one more incident from the Acts of the Apostles. Paul and Silas were arrested in Philippi, a leading city of Macedonia. After a severe beating, they were thrown into prison, where the jailer fastened them securely with chains in the innermost cell. Let's prayerfully read what follows.

> About midnight Paul and Silas were praying and singing hymns to God, and the prisoners were listening to them. Suddenly there was an earthquake, so violent that the foundations of the prison were shaken; and immediately all the doors were opened and everyone's chains were unfastened. When the jailer woke up and saw the prison doors wide open, he drew his sword and was about to kill himself, since he supposed that the prisoners had escaped. But Paul shouted in a loud voice, "Do not harm

> yourself, for we are all here." The jailer called for lights, and rushing in, he fell down trembling before Paul and Silas. Then he brought them outside and said, "Sirs, what must I do to be saved?" They answered, "Believe on the Lord Jesus, and you will be saved, you and your household." (Acts 16:25–31)

Did you notice what Paul and Silas, chained in a dark and most-likely dingy cell, were doing at midnight? Praying and singing hymns to God! (Recently when we read this passage at our daily Mass, the homilist asked us, "What would you be doing at midnight after you had had a miserable day?" A good question indeed.) Remember that Paul and Silas had been badly beaten with rods before being handed over to the jailer. The other prisoners must have been so surprised by what they were doing that they stayed awake listening to them.

In the Acts of the Apostles, reactions such as this to beatings and imprisonment are not unusual. Earlier in Jerusalem, the apostles were arrested, imprisoned, and flogged before being sent away. "As they left the council, they rejoiced that they were considered worthy to suffer dishonor for the sake of the name" (Acts 5:41). Something momentous had happened to these early Christians. The gift of the Spirit seems to have so permeated their hearts and minds that they are almost immune to suffering if it is meted out because they have been true to Jesus. They seem not to fear suffering and even death anymore. How do you account for this behavior?

I have heard of parents who have joyfully given their lives to save one of their children. I'm sure that you, too, have heard the same. Perhaps you yourself have felt this way about your own children. Well, I believe that these disciples felt that way about Jesus and God the Father. They loved God and his Son, Jesus, so much that they were ready to suffer anything, even death, to help others experience the joy of that love for God.

Notice how the actions of Paul and Silas affected the jailer: "At the same hour of the night he took them and washed their wounds; then he and his entire family were baptized without delay. He brought them up into the house and set food before them; and he and his entire household rejoiced that he had become a believer in God" (Acts 16:33–34). The jailer was transformed into a believer who acted lovingly toward his former enemies, apparently not caring about the consequences when his superiors heard of what he had done. He and his family have entered the cycle of love, prompted by the actions of Paul and Silas.

Where Are You in This Story?

In this chapter we have seen some of the effects of the life, death, and resurrection of Jesus and the outpouring of the Holy Spirit on his early followers. They were transformed from frightened, cowardly people to fearless and eloquent proclaimers of the truth about Jesus. Moreover, they offered their earliest hearers, the very ones who shouted, "Crucify him!" days ago, forgiveness and healing. Having been transformed themselves, these disciples were offering that same transformation to the enemies of Jesus.

And thousands took up that offer, so much so that the Jewish authorities became frightened of their growing numbers and began persecuting them. But the disciples of Jesus bore the blows rained on them and continued offering forgiveness and transformation to their persecutors. I have underlined in this chapter how the followers of Jesus continued what Jesus himself had done: they loved their enemies and in the process, continued the transformation of cycles of evil into cycles of good through love.

You have reflected on the Beloved Community in the early church. These people bravely played critical and transformative roles in the unfolding story of God's love for us. They participated through trying circumstances, including their own disagreements and their persecution by outside forces.

How do you see yourself as a part of our story? Do you recall times of conversion, discovery, trial, and transformation? Try to trace the impact you have had on the cycles of love and regeneration in the world around you.

9

The Story Continues

By the time all the first disciples had died, the Jesus movement had grown considerably but slowly. In *The Rise of Christianity: How the Obscure, Marginal Jesus Movement Became the Dominant Religious Force in the Western World in a Few Centuries*, sociologist Rodney Stark estimates that there were only about 7,500 Christians around AD 100, many or most of whom were Jewish converts. However, they had established house churches in many of the larger cities of the Roman Empire. Stark argues that the mission to the Jews had succeeded rather well during that first century (and for the next two), but the numbers were still quite small.

Stark studied various estimates of the number of Christians by the year 300 and then figured out that the rate of growth each decade had to be about 40 percent, which gave him these figures for the number of Christians every fifty years from the year 100: AD 100: 7,530; 150: 40,496; 200: 217,795; 250: 1,171,356; 300: 6,299,832; 350: 33,882,008. This means that Christianity grew from around 1,400 in the year 50, (a minuscule percentage of the population of the Roman Empire) to almost 34 million in the year 350—around 50 percent of the empire's population.[4]

Ongoing Effects

As I write this, our world is being ravaged by the coronavirus pandemic. Stark notes that the Roman world was decimated by two such plagues during the early centuries after the death of Jesus. Perhaps we can contemplate the following paragraphs prayerfully, keeping in mind our own experiences with the COVID-19 pandemic. During your reflections you may want to speak to God as you are moved.

In AD 165, a terrible plague, caused perhaps by smallpox, swept through the Roman Empire. During the plague's fifteen-to-twenty-year duration, a quarter to a third of the empire's population died. In 251, another plague devastated the empire, this one caused perhaps by measles. One never knew where the disease would strike. It must have been a terrifying time in which to live. This resonates with those of us who lived during the time of COVID-19, doesn't it?

Remember that medicines we take for granted were not available, and hospitals, where they existed, were rather primitive. It must have been much more chaotic for the people of that time than for us today. Try to imagine it. Sanitation was a huge problem; the streets were like running sewers; and the dead were often left on the streets. Moreover, in the cities the great majority of people lived in small, crowded spaces without much privacy at all. Stark cites data indicating that the population density of the major cities of the Roman Empire was higher than it is in the modern Indian cities of Mumbai and Kolkata. There is no way they could have practiced social distancing to curb the spread of the virus, even if they had known how the disease spread.

What Christian Love Looks Like

Now let's contemplate the impact of Christian behavior in comparison to the behavior of people of the prevailing religions in the empire. Stark maintains that the latter religions had little to offer to these suffering people. Their gods were capricious and demanding and did not seem to have any care for human beings. In addition, these religions had no real concept of a life after death to mitigate their terrible fear of death and their grief at the loss of so many loved ones. Moreover, if the priests of these religions had the means, they often left the cities for country homes with the hope that the atmosphere there would keep them safe.

Christianity, on the other hand, spoke of a God who loved his creation and the humans within it. This God so loved the world that he gave his only Son, who himself lived among us and was even killed quite cruelly; yet God still loved us. Such a God was totally different from the gods of the prevailing religions. In addition, God promised that death would not be the end of everything. In fact, God's Son was brought back to life, and that resurrected life was on offer to all who believed in him. Christians had a belief system that could and did mitigate the fear of death and the grief at the loss of loved ones. Hence, Christianity was a more attractive alternative than the other religions.

Does your own belief in Jesus give you comfort during the pandemic? Perhaps you want to speak with God about your thoughts and reactions.

More germane to the theme of this book, however, are features of Christianity as distinct from the other religions. As we know, Christians were urged to love their neighbors and even their enemies. This injunction ran counter to the prevailing ethos. According to sources cited by Stark, pity and compassion were often enough considered pathological. Christianity begins with God who is love and compassion, who loves all that he creates. Belief in this God, for Jews and Christians, entails love of God and neighbor.

We are created as images of God, and we are thus asked to act as God does. Jesus upped the ante when he urged his followers to love their enemies and even those who hate and hurt them, because that's what God does. These concepts were wholly alien in the Mediterranean area. The differences showed themselves starkly during these epidemics, when the pagans who could do so escaped from the cities but the Christians, even those who were well-to-do, stayed. In addition, many Christians cared not only for their own families and fellow Christians but also for their neighbors who were pagan. As is happening during our pandemic, those who cared for others often caught the disease, and many lost their lives as a result.

This behavior did not escape the notice of the pagans who survived the epidemics. Stark cites the words of Emperor Julian, known as the Apostate, who hated Christians, whom he called "Galileans" in the following quote: "The impious Galileans support not only their poor, but ours as well, everyone can see that our people lack aid from us."[5]

It is known that people who are cared for when ill, even if that care does not use any medicines, survive at a much higher rate than those who have no care. Sure enough, in these epidemics, Christians and their neighbors survived at a higher rate than did the pagans. As a result, the pagans wanted to know more about this new religion, and the rest is history.

You will have noticed that the Christians practiced what Jesus did and taught. They loved one another and also their pagan neighbors. They faced the darkness of terrible plagues with love for their fellow human beings. They did not contribute to the crumbling of societal norms and community; instead, they contributed care and love for others and thus fostered community. The result was that people fostered cycles of love and good rather than cycles of disintegration and hate.

Perhaps you are reminded of some of the heroic acts of love that have characterized the reactions of so many during our own pandemic. Think of the doctors and nurses from around the United States who volunteered to help in the hardest hit areas of New York City. I think of Donnell Singleton, an African American restaurant owner in Boston's

Roxbury area, whose story was told in the *Boston Globe* Metro section for June 17, 2020. With the help of activist Monique Cannon-Grant, Mr. Singleton decided to close his restaurant in order to provide meals to the hungry people of his area on a daily basis. When the demand got too great for his small space, the two of them transitioned to a free community food-delivery service. Other volunteers joined them, and by the middle of June 2020 they had delivered 70,000 meals to 800 homes in a poor area of Boston. God's Spirit works to move many people to love their neighbors, known and unknown, during times of crisis. How do you react to these characters and events in God's grand story? What acts of love have you noticed during the pandemic? Perhaps you have something to say to God or to ask God.

Some other Christian practices also contributed to the growth of Christianity. Abortion and infanticide, especially the killing of infant girls, were regularly practiced in the empire. As a result, Stark notes, the population of the empire gradually decreased and needed the infusion of other peoples to continue. Within the empire the ratio of males to females tilted dramatically so that males far exceeded females.

Christians did not practice infanticide or abortion. And so their population increased. Christian women were treated with more respect and dignity than their pagan counterparts. Indeed, women, at least in the early days, played a rather prominent role in Christian communities. This attracted women to Christianity, and their pagan husbands often enough converted as well.

Christian communities made every effort to be inclusive. The cities of the Roman Empire were composed of people from many different classes, cultures, nations, and races. Because of the teachings of Jesus about loving one another and being one in mind and heart, Christian communities tried not to divide along class, ethnic, or racial lines. Thus Christian communities provided an alternative to the rivalries and enmities that, according to Stark, prevailed in the cities. These enmities led to various areas of a city being divided by ethnic or racial identity. It was dangerous for someone from one group to go into an area belonging to a rival group. Indeed, Stark writes that one of the chief miseries for the people of the Roman Empire "was the cultural chaos produced by the crazy quilt of ethnic diversity and blazing hatreds entailed thereby. In uniting its empire, Rome created economic and political unity at the cost of cultural chaos."[6] Christian communities were a welcome alternative.

When plagues wiped out networks of people who supported one another, Christian communities offered companionship to people who were looking for such companionship and not finding it elsewhere. Christians tried to live as one community though composed of people of many races, cultures, and nationalities. Love for one another builds an inclusive community. I wonder if the churches of the West have lost, to some degree, this openness to the ethnic and racial other and, as a result, have lost much of their spiritual energy. What do you think? Maybe you are moved to talk to God about your thoughts and reactions to this section.

Where Are You in This Story?

Stark sums up his book by stating his thesis as follows: "Central doctrines of Christianity prompted and sustained attractive, liberating, and effective social relations and organizations"[7] Christians lived out the teachings of Jesus about love of one another and even of enemies. Thus Christianity offered a new identity that did not remove ethnic and racial diversity but submerged these identities under that of child of God. If my primary identity is being a child of God, and

I believe that everyone else in the world is also a child of God, then the field of play, as it were, is leveled. Then I am part of a "we," and that "we" covers everyone. Such a belief system transforms my whole way of life. Belief, like love, is shown in deeds, not just in words. Stark's final words make this point strongly: "Finally, what Christianity gave to its converts was nothing less than their humanity. In this sense virtue *was* its own reward."[8]

These early Christians, by their actions as images of God, changed the world around them for the better. They did what Jesus did, faced the chaotic and often evil cycles of the world in which they lived, and transformed them into cycles or patterns of organization and mutual care that made Christianity very attractive. They were following in the footsteps of Jesus, cooperating with God in the transformation of the world into the kingdom of God. *With the help of the Holy Spirit they created communities that propagated love rather than hatred and violence. In a sense, the contagion they spread was the contagion of love, not the contagion of sin and death.*

I'm sure that these communities were not perfect; the Beloved Community is always an endangered species, needing the vigilance of its members to remain true to itself. The fact of endangerment and even failures should not keep us from continuing to appreciate what Christians of old have done and to follow their example and the example of Jesus. God does need us, once he has created the world as it is, to bring about God's dream from the beginning of time, a world where human beings live in harmony with God, with one another, and with the whole of creation.

God's dream—the divine story—of the world continues. Your story continues also. How do you see yourself involved with the Beloved Community?

10

We Are Key Characters in a Divine Plot

We have followed God's grand story of the world. We have reflected on that story and prayed to be drawn into deeper friendship with God and to become more active, positive participants in the story that is greater than us but that has always included us. Let's continue our prayerful reflection as we look at the whole of this divine drama and the part we might play in it.

We Began as Created in God's Image

In the course of these prayerful reflections, we have seen that to be God's friend means to accept who we are by the very fact of being created in this world of ours. We are images of God, who mysteriously is three in one. God is relationship, is friendship, quite apart from anything God creates. We who are images of God, therefore, are made for relationships, made for friendship with God and with all that God creates.

All of God's creatures are in some way images of the Creator; perhaps this is why everything in this universe is related to everything else and depends on everything else. As noted earlier, other creatures in our world don't have any choice except to be trees or roses or fish or birds. They, too, need to cooperate to live and flourish, but they do this seemingly without choice, at least as far as we can determine. Human beings must choose to act as creatures made in God's image; this is the price and glory of freedom. As you engaged with me during the reading of this book, we were given the chance to be drawn more deeply into choosing to be who we are: images of God created for friendship with God, with all other humans, and with the whole of creation.

In creating us as we are, God has asked us to cooperate consciously with God in bringing about God's dream for creation. God has put great trust in us that we will choose to be who we are created to be. In effect, our choice is between being inhuman or human. In other words, God is not putting an added burden on us by asking us to cooperate in building up the kingdom of God and living out the grand story of creation; God is simply asking us to be who we are created to be. But we must choose to be human, not inhuman. This was the point Rodney Stark made in the lines cited in the last chapter: "Finally, what Christianity gave to its converts was nothing less than their humanity. In this sense virtue *was* its own reward."[9] God, in creating us, gave us a chance to be human, which means to be humane, compassionate, loving, and creative, rather than their opposites.

What we are asked to do, with God's help, is foster cycles of positive development in our world that move us toward God's dream. Here are some examples of such positive cycles. Parents care for their children and raise them to be caring, responsible, and humane citizens of our world, and the children do the same for their children. When neighbors are in need, we help them, and they, in turn, help others. We gather in organizations of varying size and complexity to foster a better life for everyone, and these organizations live beyond their creators to continue to do good.

When I mentioned cycles of love, I was referring to these and other ways in which humans have used their gifts to move the world toward the kingdom of God. Such cycles of love are fostered by God's Spirit, who is constantly trying to turn our hearts and minds toward acting to bring about the Beloved Community.

Given the enormous problems we face in our country and world, some forms of corporate endeavor are the only way we can make a difference. In fact, if we do not think cooperatively, the temptation will be to throw up our hands in despair and be content to leave the big picture to the very corporate structures and institutions that have brought us to the dire straits the world now faces. The question we must answer is, How can we mobilize ourselves to try to bring about a more just and caring society in our communities and countries?

Do these summary paragraphs ring a bell with you? Are the ideas becoming part of your own way of thinking and praying? Are you noticing a change in your way of acting? Maybe you feel the urge to have a chat with God about these matters.

Because of Sin, Humanity Became a Nemesis in God's Story

Scripture tells us stories to indicate how sin and evil entered God's good creation. Humans chose not to trust God but to try to control their own destinies apart from God. Instead of continuing as friends of God, we became enemies. We chose not to accept who we are, creatures created for friendship and cooperation with God. In fact, we ended up working against God in many ways.

The effects of our inhumanity are all around us, as we know from experience and have seen in the Scripture stories throughout this book. Humans have introduced cycles of decline and evil that run counter to what God wants in our world. We have looked at such cycles both in biblical times and in early Christian times. Let's reflect prayerfully on our own world to see how these cycles of decline work themselves out now.

Conflicts in the Plot

The COVID-19 pandemic has brought to our consciousness rather forcefully the consequences of economic inequality in the United States and in other parts of the world. The hardest-hit communities in the United States are those of African Americans and Hispanics, which have borne the effects of this economic inequality at a rate much higher than their percentage of the population. The United States is by far the richest country in the world, but these communities have not shared in the prosperity in any way proportionate to their numbers or their contributions to society. In addition, they often do not have adequate health coverage; thus, they suffer from various underlying conditions, which make them much more vulnerable to the virus.

As I write, people in these communities are dying of COVID-19 at a much higher rate than are members of other racial and ethnic communities. You could say that the present situation is the product of a society that over a long period of time did not and does not care for all its members in an equal and healthy way. Here is an example of a cycle of decline that is the result of human sinfulness.

In countries of what is called the developing world, poverty within the vast majority of the population has made that majority extremely susceptible to the pandemic. For years we in the developed world have been told about this poverty, but we have not mustered the nerve and the energy to change our way of life that is so dependent on the underpaid labor and the resources available in countries of the developed world. This is yet another example of a human-caused cycle of decline from what God wants in our world.

How do you react to these realities? Do they make sense to you? Do you see more clearly how downward spirals do exist in our world and how they run counter to what God dreams for our world? How can we—created in God's image—help transform the cycles of decline that have led to such enormous disparities in the distribution of the goods of this world? Perhaps more practically the question should be, How can we mobilize into groups to be effective forces of social change in our world? Can we join groups or organizations that foster a different economic model that is more in line with the teachings of Jesus? How does my being a friend of God influence how I vote and how I spend my money? These and other questions might come to mind as you ponder the deleterious effects of our economic and political system on immigrants and people of color.

When the killing of George Floyd, an unarmed African American man, by a white police officer, was caught on camera and went viral, many citizens of the United States became aware of the racism that pervades our nation. What was dawning on more and more white Americans is the pervasive racism in this country, which Jim Wallis called America's original sin, a sin that started in 1619 when the first slave ship brought Africans here to serve the white economy. The evil of slavery has spawned a history of racial injustice and murder in the United States that can only be called a cycle of sin and evil. Here again we see how evil begets evil in a downward cycle until we face it with God's help and transform it into something else. Notice, too, how the most effective recent protest movements against racial injustice were both multiracial and nonviolent.

The Divine Plot: How God Overcomes These Cycles of Decline

Repeatedly in the Bible and in the early history of Christianity, we have seen that God responds to evil with love and asks us to cooperate in the transformation of evil by love. God continually forgives humans who have turned away from his friendship and brings them back into that friendship and trusts them to become human. The Bible can be read as a story of God's faithful love of us humans who continually fail to be the friends of God we are created to be.

God chose Abraham and Sarah and their descendants as his special people to be light for the world, a community and nation founded on solidarity and justice for all to keep alive in our world who God is and what God wants for the good of all humanity. The history of the Israelites reveals the same history of God's fidelity to his friendship with them, and their spotty record as friends of God. Yet God never gave up on his love for us and our world. If we are honest, we would have to admit that Christians have had a record at least as spotty as did the Israelites in acting like people made in God's image. Our Christian churches seem filled with warring factions and bitter enmities to this day.

Because I am a Christian and am writing for Christians, I have stressed the Bible and its long story. But God is not a tribal god; God is the creator of everything and everyone that exists. The Bible even tells the story such that every human being is descended from two ancestors, Adam and Eve. Thus, the Bible wants us to know that all human beings belong to one family: the family of God.

But as the human race has grown, we have spread across the planet. Because God creates all of us for friendship with God, God must have been working with all of us to draw all into friendship with God and cooperation in bringing about God's dream in our world. We should expect to find throughout human history instances of people being inspired to act as images of God and thus cooperate with God. I would not want us to think that Christians alone have a corner on the market of what it means to be human beings and friends of God. As mentioned earlier, even the Bible notes how non-Jews and non-Christians have acted for the good of the whole and thus cooperated with God.

In these final pages I want to offer some thoughts and reflections on what all our considerations in this book have to do with the lives we actually live. As you prayed and reflected with me over these pages, you must have felt the tug of, and perhaps the fear of, God's hopes and desires for you. Let's make the tug explicit from here to the end. You may feel challenged, nervous, put off, or perhaps even angry as you read. Pay attention to your reactions and take some time to reflect with God about them to see what reactions are from God or lead toward God and what reactions are not from God and lead to self-absorption and self-justification or resentment. By paying attention in this way, you will be able to discern what leads you to greater faith, hope, and love, greater peace and hope for our future. Also, you will be growing closer to God in your prayer and in your life.

I will ask you to look prayerfully with me at various areas of our present life to see what it might mean to be and act more like an image of God in our world. In a sense, we will together be making a moral inventory of ourselves in relation to what God hopes for us. Because I can't discuss every area of life in which we are asked to become protagonists in God's grand story of the world, take these thoughts as the tip of the iceberg; these do not by any means cover everything, nor could they. I hope that these prayerful reflections will help you examine your own life and its possibilities for changing cycles of decline into cycles of movement toward the fulfillment of God's dream for you and for the world.

Family and Friends

How do we act as images of God with those who are closest to us, those in our families and those who are our close friends? I suggest that you take some time to reflect prayerfully about your interactions with the members of your immediate and extended family. Ask God to help you look honestly at how you interact with each of them. Do you notice in your family how love was passed on from one person to others with positive effects? Were you the recipient of such love? If you do notice such love, then you have a personal example of how cycles of love happen and have a positive impact on the world around us. I hope that you thanked the people who brought light and love into your life and the lives of others close to you.

You might also ask yourself if you have been a source of light and love for others close to you. If you have been such a source, have others thanked you? How did you feel? If we notice how we feel when others thank us, we may be more likely to thank others. If some of those we thought of as points of light are now dead, we could thank them as a prayer.

Did you notice any indications of the opposite of a loving cycle, for example, instances of active dislike or dysfunction in the family? Some of these may have occurred before you were born, but they still had an effect even after those responsible died, because you know something of what they did or said that affected the family. You know then, from experience, how sinful acts keep on giving, as it were, just as good acts do. Perhaps you have remembered how you yourself have been a source of dysfunction in your family or close circle of friends. How did it come about? Did you notice how any of your actions or words might have caused a split in the family or circle of friends?

If you are aware of having some antipathy or resentment toward someone in your family or friends, you might want to try something that has helped me. Every day during my morning prayer, I include something like this: "Help me today to meet everyone with openness and affection rather than suspicion and fear," and then I name those for whom I do not have affection. This prayer has improved my reactions and behavior for the better.

This might be a good place to introduce three of the 12 Steps of Alcoholics Anonymous because they touch on how to notice our missteps and how to deal with those that have affected others.

4. Made a searching and fearless moral inventory of ourselves. . . .

8. Made a list of all persons we had harmed, and became willing to make amends to them all.

9. Made direct amends to such people wherever possible, except when to do so would injure them or others.

Alcoholics and other addicts who follow the spirituality of AA realize that many of their actions have hurt others and that the path to recovery requires recognizing their moral failings and making amends for them. Since you may have become aware of how your actions or words have caused harm in your family or circle of friends, you may want to make amends to those you have hurt, as far as this is possible.

If you recognize that you are estranged from a family member or former friend because of something you or the other or others have done, you might want to ask God's help to see how you can restore what was lost by asking for forgiveness or by forgiving, depending on who was at fault. Perhaps the fault was mutual; then it might be possible to take the first step to see if the ties can be restored.

You can see that becoming an active participant in God's story, cooperating with God to bring about God's dream, can be costly. However, I can assure you from personal experience that it's well worth the effort involved when right relations are restored. You will feel a great relief, I'm sure, and God will be smiling.

When I told my friend Sr. Carol Johannes, O.P., about this book, she wrote back the following, which fits well with what we have just been discussing:

> Speaking of transforming cycles of evil into cycles of love, I came across a nice definition of the work of forgiveness in doing our workshop on aging. In the book *From Age-ing to Sage-ing*, Rabbi Zalman Schachter-Shalomi writes, "The critical role of forgiveness is challenging us with the evolutionary task of ennobling our sufferings, transmuting suffering and sorrow into understanding and the capacity to love."[10] I find that statement to be a keeper.

So do I.

While we're reflecting on forgiveness, I want to mention how often African Americans have forgiven those who injured them or killed their loved ones. After Dylann Roof killed six members of the Charleston, South Carolina, Emanuel AME church during a Bible study on June 17, 2015, the family members of the victims told Mr. Roof that they forgave him. In Boston, three-year-old Kai Leigh Harriott was shot and paralyzed by a stray bullet fired by

Anthony Warren. Three years later at Warren's trial, she forgave him, as did her family. Her forgiveness moved Mr. Warren to change his life and, in prison, move toward a life more caring for others. These are just two examples of such generosity inspired by God's Spirit. Such examples indicate that it is possible to forgive even heinous crimes. Such crimes do not have to have the last word; God's Spirit can stop the cycle of violence from continuing—can turn around the story's plot—by inspiring forgiveness.

Tough Love

Too often people think that Christian love means suffering in silence while being physically or emotionally abused. The mention of the 12 Steps of AA reminds me of the phrase *tough love*, which is often associated with AA practice. Some prayerful reflection on this theme is in order here as we speak of how evil is transformed by love.

Alcoholic behavior can disrupt a family and a workplace with deleterious consequences that have a downward spiraling effect on everyone involved. Often the behavior goes on for years, and no one takes the risk of naming the elephant in the room. In addition, all of us have probably heard of abused spouses who have been counseled by a priest or minister to bear the burden, with the idea of doing what Jesus did on the cross. Such advice is alien, I believe, to what Jesus was about. Allowing the abuse to go on does no one any good. What God wants is to transform evil through love. Tough love is often the only way to do this.

In AA practice, tough love is associated often with facing someone who is misusing alcohol, but with a loving honesty about the facts of what drinking alcohol is doing not only to the alcoholic but also to those around him or her. The preferred method is to do an intervention with a small group of people who care about the alcoholic and who have been affected by that person's behavior. Here the emphasis is on telling the person the facts that you have noticed: for example, slurring of speech, drunken outbursts, the large amounts of alcohol consumed. It would also include talking about how the drinking and the behavior associated with it are affecting you and your relationship with the person. What we are asked to avoid is using terms that stigmatize or belittle the other, such as *alkie* or *junkie*. Even if we have to say hard things to the other, we need to say them with love and care.

If the bad behavior must stop, then tough love also must include an "or else." For example, "If you don't take steps to address the issue, then you have to leave my (our) house." A friend of mine told me that she would not continue our friendship if I did not do something about my drinking. Such tough love can be as tough on the one giving the "or else" as it is for the one receiving it. But this kind of tough love is necessary to stop cycles of decline that are caused by people's bad behavior. Do you see how such acts of tough love may be the only hope of transforming a cycle of decline into a cycle of positive development not only for the other person but also for many others with whom that person will interact in the future? (An aside: people who need help with how to go about such an intervention can get this help from the website americanaddictioncenters.org, which offers a step-by-step guide.)

The same tough-love approach may be needed if a spouse or partner is emotionally or physically abusive. In such a case the abused spouse or partner may have to go to the police to get a restraining order to stop the abuse. Eventually a separation or divorce may be necessary. That's tough love, but it is love. Abusive treatment of others is not to be tolerated. The abused spouse who takes action to stop it is, in fact, doing the other a favor.

What I have just written about tough love may come in handy in dealing with people who have a bad effect on the environment in a family or workplace. For example, once when I was a superior, I got into a funk because of something that happened in our relatively small community. As a result, without my awareness, I was having a deleterious effect on the whole community because the others picked up my attitude. One of the community members took me aside and told me in a kind and honest way the effect of my current disposition. As a result of his intervention, I realized what was going on in me and asked God's help to change my inner state. God obliged. The community member had such an effect because he approached me not with anger or condemnation but with a caring-yet-honest statement of the deleterious effect my feelings were having on the community.

Does what I have written here make sense to you? Are you reminded of situations where tough love changed lives? Does it scare you to think that you may be called upon to offer tough love to others? It scares me too. But perhaps that is something you want to talk over with God.

I want to introduce a poem here, written by the Pulitzer Prize–winning poet Franz Wright, who was my friend the last few years of his relatively short life. Franz lived through a lot of psychic and physical pain, but he did find God, and in finding God, he found hope. He was no stranger to tough love. The poem speaks directly to the theme of this book, especially in its last lines. The poem is called "The Hawk." Perhaps it will speak to you as it did to me of love of neighbor.

> Maybe in a million years
> a better form of human
> being will come, happier
> and more intelligent. A few already
> have infiltrated this world and lived
> to very much regret it,
> I suppose.
> Me,
> I'd prefer to have come
> in the form of that hawk, floating over
> the mirroring fire
> of Clearlake's
> hill, my gold
> skull filled with nothing
> but God's will
> the whole day through, instead
> of these glinting voices incessantly
> unerringly guiding me
> to pursue
> what makes me sick, and not to
> what makes me glad. And yet
> I am changing: this three-pound lump
> of sentient meat electrified

by hope and terror has learned to hear
His silence like the sun,
And sought to change!
And friends
on earth at the same time
as me, listen: from the sound of those crickets
last night, René Char said
prenatal life
must have been sweet—
each voice perhaps also a star
in that night
from which
this time
we won't be
interrupted anymore—but
fellow monsters while we are still here, for one
minute, think
about this: there is someone right now who is
looking
to you, not Him, for whatever
love still exists.[11]

And remember that God wants us to show love, sometimes tough love, to that someone.

Places of Work or of Congregating with Others

Have you ever examined your behavior at work or in other organizations to which you belong? Here, too, we are being asked by God to act as people made in the divine image, to be carriers of good—rather than bad—feelings. Here, too, we can be cooperators with God in developing an atmosphere that makes the workplace or organization a welcoming and enjoyable place to be, or we can contribute to an atmosphere that makes the place toxic, a place everyone wants to leave as soon as possible. Perhaps as you prayerfully read and reflect on the following stories, you may be prodded to examine your own manner and behavior as you go about daily routines.

Once I was in a car driven by a young lawyer. I was amazed at his generosity in greeting people. As we drove through a toll booth, he took time to say hello to the collector and to wish him a good day. When we got to the office building where we had some business, he greeted everyone we met with an openness and kindness that were contagious. I felt that I had met someone imbued with the Spirit of Jesus who helped foster an atmosphere of friendliness wherever he went.

In an essay in his posthumously published collection of best essays, *One Long River of Song*, Brian Doyle begins this way: "Had a brief chat with God the other day. This was at the United States post office. God was manning the counter from one to five, as he does every blessed day." He then goes on to describe how this post office clerk handled his customers all the time. Doyle talks about the man's patience, even with customers who were angry and abusive. Doyle asked him how he did it and got these replies: "I try to put myself in their position" or "Witnessing vented emotion is part of the job" or "All storms blow over" or "We are all neighbors in the end." The clerk even makes a note if the customer who is abusive has a valid point that ought to be addressed by the post office. He seems to know every regular customer's name, even the names of their dogs. Near the end of the essay Doyle writes, "If we cannot see God in the vessels into which the electricity of astonishing life is poured by a profligate creation, vessels like this wonderfully and eternally gracious gentleman at the Post Office, then we are very bad at the religion we claim to practice." He ends with the following words:

> So it is that I have seen God at the United States Post Office, and spoken to him, and been edified and elevated by his grace, which slakes all those who thirst, which is each of us, which is all of us.[12]

Don't these stories touch you and make you want to be such an inspiring protagonist in God's grand story wherever you work or live? Think of how my lawyer friend and this postal clerk spread a contagion of warmth and, may I say, love to everyone they meet. That contagion cannot help but shift the moods of many, many others and thus help make their small part of the world a better place. We see how the harmony God wants fans out across the world.

In our workplaces, communities, and organizations, we run into systemic instances of a cycle of evil or decline, such as racial inequality, or practices that are wasteful of increasingly scarce resources, or illegal or immoral practices that go unaddressed. We need to consider how to deal with such issues in ways that are Godlike, knowing that those who call attention to such systemic issues might be penalized themselves. I can't leave this section without noting how crucial it is to address such practices if ever we are to have a just and moral society more worthy of what God intends with the creation of us human beings.

As I was writing this section, I was also reading Brian Doyle's *Eight Whopping Lies and Other Stories of Bruised Grace*. He tells a moving story of how a corporation acted toward families of eighty-three employees who were murdered in the attack on the South Tower of the World Trade

Center on September 11, 2011. The story is called "The Children of Sandler O'Neill." Sandler O'Neill was an investment banking firm with offices in five of the largest cities in the United States. In the days that followed this tragedy, the company decided to pay the families of the deceased the full salaries including bonuses to the end of the year; their families were kept on full employee benefits for the next ten years; and the company helped set up a foundation to pay for college for all seventy-six children of those murdered. Doyle gives some of the details of how many of these children have finished college, but what most interested me (and Doyle) was why the company did it. He talked with the founder of the company, Jimmy Dunne, and asked him. Here is what Dunne answered.

> Because there was a moment in time to stand up. . . . Because we believed at that moment that what happens from now will echo for a hundred years in the families of our people, their kids and their grandkids. Because I knew that how we conducted ourselves in those first few hours and days would define who we really were and what we were about. Because I knew that this was the critical hour, and if we just got by without being honorable, then we stood for nothing.[13]

Isn't that a remarkable statement? Here's a man who acted as a true hero of the story—a person made in the divine image—whether he was conscious of it or not, and who was part of a corporation that did the right thing at a very difficult time. You will have noticed that Mr. Dunne was well aware of how good and bad actions have repercussions down the ages. When evil struck, Sandler O'Neill started a cycle of good to counteract it.

Here's an example of how a man I know dealt with a cycle of evil. I have changed the circumstances to hide the identity of all concerned. This man, let's say, was the CEO of a large corporation in a medium-sized city. He tried to make decisions that fostered the good of the institution and its employees. At one point he was faced with a powerful figure on the board of the corporation who wanted him to make a decision that would profit another organization rather than the corporation he headed. The pressure was enormous, but he held his ground against that pressure because he believed the other action would be wrong. As I listened to him telling me the story, I thought that this man had faced evil and did not allow himself to be swayed by it. God, I told him, "must have been very happy with you."

The Opposite of the Novel *Lord of the Flies*

In William Golding's *Lord of the Flies*, a group of English schoolboys are stranded on a desert island and rather quickly descend into chaos and cruelty. Our culture tends toward believing that this novel depicts human reality. The prevailing sentiment is that we live in a dog-eat-dog world, as it were; hence, you can't trust anyone. If you watch the evening news on television, you know that most of the news presented could be seen to fit this pessimistic sentiment. I think that the people who deliver these news editions know this and that is why they try to end the daily dose of bad news with some good news to brighten our spirits a little. But is the pessimism actually true to life? Given what we have been reflecting on in this book, it seems, at the least, unduly pessimistic.

Does this pessimistic expectation fit your own experience? Ask God's help to examine some recent weeks in your life and then remember some of the things that have happened or that you have heard of. When you are satisfied with that prayer, ask yourself if your experience matches the pessimism of our culture.

My lawyer friend and Brian Doyle's postal clerk belie the pessimism, don't they? Jimmy Dunne of Sandler O'Neill and my friend who refused to give in to pressure also belie it. During the coronavirus pandemic, we have heard of and seen how all over the world, men and women on the front lines of community service—police, firefighters, ambulance drivers, nurses and doctors, and ordinary citizens—have risked their own health to help others. In the United States we saw medical personnel from all over the country volunteer to help out in New York City when that city became the epicenter of the outbreak of COVID-19 infections. In chapter 9 I brought up the example of Donnell Singleton, who closed his restaurant in order to feed more needy people in his neighborhood.

After the video of George Floyd's death went viral, it seemed that the whole country, and indeed the whole world, was outraged and wanted to do something to change the racism that has led to too many instances of killings like this. The marches for a change of our culture were composed of people of all races and ages. The solidarity was amazing. I saw a video in which one African American broke down in sobs as he said, "White people cared that a Black man was killed. White people cared that a Black man was killed. White people cared that a Black man was killed." We do seem to be better than William Golding painted us in his novel.

My friend Joseph Owens, SJ, put me onto the following story. The Dutch historian Rutger Bregman discovered a real-life incident that belies Golding's view of humanity. Six teenage boys from the islands of Tonga set off on a fishing trip in the 1960s, were caught in a huge storm, and were shipwrecked on a tiny remote island. They spent fifteen months on this island and were finally rescued by an Australian ship. Their days were described as follows:

> The kids agreed to work in teams of two, drawing up a strict roster for garden, kitchen, and guard duty. Sometimes they quarreled, but whenever that happened they solved it by imposing a time-out. . . . Their days began and ended with song and prayer.[14]
>
> These teenage boys cooperated and used their ingenuity together to create a type of beloved community when shipwrecked on a deserted island in the Pacific.
>
> They took someone else's boat to get away from a school life that was boring. Yet on that island God's Spirit moved them to care for one another and thus, not only to survive but to thrive.

These optimistic stories may remind us that the Spirit of God is always active in our world, trying to move the minds and hearts of human beings toward mutuality, cooperation, and care for one another. The Spirit moves us always toward creating or joining cycles of positive development. These stories are indications of the success of the Spirit's initiatives. God is on the side of development toward the Beloved Community. *Remember that. God wants this for us. We need to hold on to faith and trust in God as the antidote to any tendencies toward pessimism about the creation.*

What is your response to these stories? What stories could you tell about what happens in the world to indicate that pessimism is not the only story being told?

Some Writings That Also Help Change the World

Over the past few years I have read some novels and other books that seemed to me to be moving me and those who read them in the direction God wants. Let me just mention some of them with the hope that this section will remind you of books or music or videos that have had the same effect on you. I do this to indicate that we can be images of God no matter what our skills and talents are. In this case, it's writers who, whether they know it or not, become, through the stories they write, partners with God in the larger story.

Let me start with Brian Doyle, two of whose books I have mentioned already. He wrote many essays, but also novels and poetry. His writing is a breath of fresh air with its daring, its attention to details many of us miss, and its humor. Doyle believed in God and spoke of God and God's ways with such honesty, good humor, and solid belief that it takes your breath away at times. I have now read the posthumous collection of his essays, *One Long River of Song*, three times in the past year and passed it on to good friends. I wish he were still writing.

One of the novels I read this year is Colum McCann's *Apeirogon*. It's a novel like few others. The reader gets a wonderful story of a Palestinian and an Israeli, both of whom lost young daughters because of the Palestinian-Israeli tensions; the Palestinian's daughter was shot in the back by an Israeli soldier, and the Israeli's daughter was killed by a Palestinian suicide bomber. They became friends and cooperators in efforts to bring about peaceful relations between their two peoples. In addition to the story, the reader also gets lessons in history, in flights of birds, and other areas. The two men are real people, but McCann writes a novel to tell their story. The story is moving indeed and is a novelistic effort to move readers toward hope for our broken world and, perhaps, toward action to cooperate with what God is doing in it.

Ann Patchett's novel *Commonwealth* tells an engrossing story of two families who become intertwined because the father of one family falls in love with the mother of the other, at the baptism party for the mother's child, no less. The novel follows the members of the two families over time as they deal with the fallout from the breakup of the two marriages. As with Patchett's other novels, this one is well written and engaging, but I also noticed that I had come to care for all the characters, even the two who are the initiators of the family breakups. Clearly Ann Patchett cares for all her characters and makes none of them into monsters. I felt that this is the kind of world God wants. Not that God wants marital infidelities but rather wants evil or sin—in the novel's case, infidelity—to be transformed through love. God wants all of us humans to live out our holy purpose almost in spite of ourselves.

Ann Patchett put me onto Kate DiCamillo's novels for young people through an essay she wrote in the *New York Times Book Review*, March 30, 2020. Because of Patchett's high praise, I began reading DiCamillo's novels. All of them are skillfully crafted and engaging and show the reader how love really is what is needed in this broken world. In each novel, love changes some of her characters for the better, thus showing young people, through story, how love makes the world go 'round. As with a number of other books written with young people in mind, DiCamillo's novels do affect adults. I'm a witness to that statement.

Two of DiCamillo's novels moved me most profoundly, *The Miraculous Journey of Edward Tulane* and *Because of Winn-Dixie*. The first follows the adventures of a china rabbit who learns, through hard knocks and the help of strangers, what it means to love. Here's what I jotted when I finished the second. "A truly lovely story of how a lonely young girl finds a stray, smelly dog in a grocery store and names him after a grocery chain in the South. The dog, Winn-Dixie, leads her to a lot of friends in the new town where her father is a preacher. (Her mother left them both when Opal was three or so, probably because of alcohol and unhappiness.) I cried with joy through the last two chapters. Life, one of the characters says, 'was like a Littmus Lozenge, how the sweet and the sad were all mixed up together and how hard it was to separate them out. It was confusing.'"[15]

Of course, the poem "The Hawk" by my late friend Franz Wright is one of many poems that have also moved me in the direction of God's dream for our world.

I hope that what I have written in this section has reminded you of books or other creative works that have moved you and influenced your life for the better. Were you ever moved by a creative work—a book, poem, song, movie, painting, sculpture—to do something good that you never considered before or to take action to change your own life or some part of your world for the better? God is always working to move the world toward the dream that started creation.

Heated Conversations and Meetings

In the United States and in many other countries, conversations between people who hold opposing positions have grown increasingly heated, sometimes even violent. Earlier I mentioned how the former head of the conservative think tank American Enterprise Institute, Arthur C. Brooks, became so worried about the state of our American democracy that he wrote *Love Your Enemies: How Decent People Can Save America from the Culture of Contempt.* In that book he details the ravages of the culture of contempt and gives examples of people and groups who have done something to change this culture. A look at that book might give you some good examples of how people have overcome the prevailing ethos. Here I would just like to give some ideas for your prayerful consideration as you and I both try to do our best to cooperate with God in the redemption of the world's story.

Many years ago, I was part of a faculty that included priests, sisters, and laypeople. We were having a faculty meeting when the issue arose of why all the priests did not concelebrate at the school Masses. The talk too quickly became acrimonious, with charges and countercharges, arguments and counterarguments flying about. I felt more and more uncomfortable and saw no way out of the disagreement. To this day I do not know what possessed me, but I believe that it was the grace of God. I said something like this: "I'm a daily communicant and have been all my life. But in this school where we have so many priests, I don't feel the need to be one of the celebrating priests. The Eucharist should not divide us, as I fear is happening; it should unite us." What I did was tell my story and why I acted as I did without arguing for my position. That intervention seemed to change the way the conversation went on from there.

I was scared as I started to speak but felt impelled to do so by something or someone beyond me. I now consider that I was moved by the Spirit of God to speak of my experience in a way that did not judge anyone else. I tell the story because I am grateful to God for the inspiration, and I tell it to give us something to ponder together.

Have you noticed how telling one's story changes the tenor of a conversation in a positive way? I am reminded of how Peter quieted the angry queries of the Jewish-Christian leaders of the community in Jerusalem when they heard that he had entered a Gentile's house, baptized the Gentiles, and ate with them. Peter simply told them what happened. At the Council in Jerusalem, Peter again told his story and was joined by Paul, who told his story, and a difference that could have split the early Christians was settled by not laying new burdens on Gentile converts.

How do you react to this section? Does it make sense to you? Raise questions? Does it give you something to ponder and pray over?

Arguments about Politics and Other Disputed Topics

I'm sure that you have noticed how difficult conversations about politics and social issues have become in the United States and, it seems, in many other countries. Let's spend a little time reflecting prayerfully on this topic. Remember our mode of operation throughout. Here we ask God to help us act as images of God with those who have deeply held opinions different from ours. In effect, we are asking help to be part of God's work in transforming the culture of contempt into a culture of communal respect.

I might add that the culture of contempt has also affected discourse in the churches. I am familiar with the Roman Catholic Church and can attest that we have been badly affected. Many arguments devolve into anathemas and cries of heresy from both sides. Although I will be using our political dialogue in the United States as the example, those of us affected by the same culture in our church can easily transfer the principles to our way of operating.

What can we do to change this situation? *How can I change a culture?* I think, and I realize that you are probably asking the same question. Well, we begin with reality; we cannot change the culture by ourselves. But we have to start somewhere. So, let it begin with me and you.

Before we move on, why don't you ask God's help to notice your own reactions to what is going on in our country's political and social life. Perhaps you can ask God for his reactions to our situation. When you have finished, you may find my own reflections helpful.

Let's start with our attitudes toward those who disagree with us on things about which we both feel deeply. You might start with the most polarizing figure in our country right now: President Trump. I realize that he may not be our president by the time this book reaches you, but as I write, he is the most polarizing figure. How do you feel about him and his followers? How do you feel about those who are strongly against him and his policies? Be honest with yourself. Can you see yourself having a civilized and open conversation with those who disagree with you about him, a conversation that might not change either party's convictions but which would leave you both feeling some respect and even liking for one another?

About a year ago, I realized that I had such strong feelings on this topic that I avoided talking about politics except with like-minded friends. The danger was that I would avoid the "others" if I could. I asked God to help me not to avoid "them" and to not be so caught up in this culture of contempt. I no longer avoid them, and I have begun to have sympathy for them. I'm still a work in progress in this area and, indeed, in many others.

The one thing that's clear to me is that God does not have contempt for anyone. This means that we who are God's images need to clean up our act, as it were, with God's help. That may take some time, once we start looking honestly at ourselves. But it's necessary. One way forward on this point is to let God love us with all our warts and moles and sins. If we realize deeply that we are loved sinners, then it can't help but make us more willing to give the "other" the same slack God gives us.

I cannot stress this point enough. If we try to be "good" Christians without that profound sense and belief that we are the beloved of God, sinners though we all are, we will fail badly. We cannot do it on our own; and we cannot do it without knowing in our bones that we are loved, warts and all. We will never approach being images of God's love unless we are wrapped in that love ourselves. Only then can we hope to have contempt for no one.

When wrapped in that love, we may then be able to engage in helpful conversations with those who disagree with us on issues that are neuralgic for both of us. For one thing, we might be willing to ask the other to explain why they have such a strong opinion about, say, Mr. Trump. This might then lead to a fruitful conversation about what both of us care about. Through this conversation we might even find common ground and realize that we can work together from that vantage point, or we might just agree to disagree and not let this disagreement mean permanent estrangement. The one thing I am sure about is that we can move forward together only if we come to care for one another and for the common good and realize that the common good must include everyone or it is neither common nor good.

My friend Tim Kochems, a psychologist and psychoanalyst, recently wrote an essay in *Voices*, the journal of the American Academy of Psychotherapists, that is an example of how to engage in a conversation on a difficult subject and be an image of God. Tim tells his fellow psychotherapists that while he loves being a psychotherapist, he has never felt at home with them. All his life, he writes, he has felt a call deeper than any other call, and that is a call to love. He labels this call the thread of love. This deeper thread runs through all parts of his life, including psychotherapy. He loves his clients. When he tries to talk about this deeper thread, he finds his colleagues get distant and sometimes argumentative. Throughout the essay Tim just tells his story; he does not argue for his point of view, nor does he disparage his colleagues. For me this was a model of how to tell the truth with love. (The essay is in *Voices*, Spring 2020, 55–60.)

I realize that I have only touched the surface of this topic, but we have to begin someplace. As the peace hymn says, "Let there be peace on earth, and let it begin with me." None of us alone can change the world, but I am encouraged when I read something that Krista Tippett wrote:

> Still, I am dazzled by the great good I can discern everywhere out there. . . . I have a heart full, arms full, a mind brimful and bursting with a sense of what is healing us even as I write, even when we don't know it and haven't asked for it. And I do mean healing: not curing, not solving, not fixing, but creating the opportunity for deepened life together, for growing more wise and more whole, not just older, not just smarter.[16]

Tippett is speaking of the number of points of light occurring in our world where people are "creating the opportunity for deepened life together." I'm hoping that this book will be a catalyst for the creation of more such points of light. Let's grow "more wise and more whole" together. Let's join together in God's great work!

How do you react to this section? Once again, I urge you to spend time with God conversing about your reactions and thoughts and reservations.

Racism

Recent events have brought home to a majority of Americans how much African Americans still suffer the effects of racism that sits deeply in most white people. First, let's thank God for the fact that we white Americans seem to be growing more and more conscious of the racism in our country and its disastrous effects on the lives of people of color and especially of African Americans. I do not need to rehearse the signs of that growing awareness here. What I hope is that you will want to participate in the efforts to root out racism in yourself and others. We are all infected with this "original sin" of the United States of America. How do we go about rooting it out? We need God's help to answer that question. Right now, let's ask God for that help and then prayerfully reflect with God on ourselves. Our purpose here is not to make us feel ashamed and guilty but to see the truth of ourselves so that we can ask God to help us be transformed.

Do we know well any people of color? If not, why not? If we do not, it may be a sign of how segregated our life is and then lead us to wonder why this is so. If we do know people of color, we can ask ourselves how well we know them. Do we know anything about their families? Their lives? Their experience of life in the United States? If we don't know any of these personal details, then perhaps it indicates that we do not have a personal relationship with them. You might ask yourself why this is so.

Have you ever spoken with an African American, for example, about whether they have experienced racial profiling from the police or from fellow citizens? Have you ever asked an African American father or mother how they feel when their children leave the house alone? I could go on, but you probably get my point.

Many if not most of us white Americans have not had close personal relationships with people of color. One of the things that inhibits friendships between races, I believe, is fear. We fear the "other." African Americans have good reasons to fear white Americans; they have experienced the effects of our racism all their lives. I suspect that the fears of us white people are most probably based on fear of the unknown. The only remedy for such fear is for us to get to know one another as persons, as real neighbors, and, in time, even as friends.

What most changed my life in this regard was being asked to correspond with a prisoner who turned out be African American. Darrell Jones was sentenced to life without parole for a murder he did not commit. I didn't know this or his race when I was told that a prisoner wanted to correspond with someone who was a psychologist and a believer. In the third or fourth letter I received from Darrell, he asked, "Do you know that I'm African American?" Tears came to my eyes when I realized that he thought I would not want to write to him if I knew this. The fact that he asked the question spoke volumes to me of how racism had affected him. My relationship with Darrell has deepened over the many years since then. He now calls me Dad, and I look on him as the son I never thought to have. As a result, too, I have gotten to know his family and friends. Darrell's conviction was overturned, one of the reasons for the ruling being racial bias in a juror. A year and a half later, in a retrial, Darrell was found not guilty by a jury of his peers. I wept along with his friends, Black and white, Christian and Muslim and Jew.

I know that I have not written all that much in this section, but I don't feel that I have much more to offer except to ask you to join me in being part of the solution to our country's original sin: white supremacy, which has led to slavery, inequality, violence, and terrorism against non-whites. We all need to work together with God to achieve this healing.

How do you react to this section? I hope you will engage with God and perhaps with others in the conversations that are necessary for this healing.

Militarism and Nonviolence

Those of us who are citizens of the United States and also Christian are in a difficult situation. Our nation has the most powerful military in the world and is also the world's leading manufacturer and seller of arms of all kinds to other nations. In addition, the United States has more weapons in the hands of more citizens than any other country in the world. It would not surprise me to hear that our economy would crater if the United States were to decrease its military forces significantly and stop making weapons of all sorts. Yet Christ calls us to love our enemies. What are we who want to live as images of God and other Christs to do in this situation? I believe that all of us need to be willing to look honestly at this issue.

Wars will never bring about the end of all war; nor will weapons in our houses bring us peace of mind. I believe that Jesus saw clearly the truths of these two sentences; that's why he was so insistent on his followers loving one another, their neighbors, and even their enemies. I don't know how to help you face this issue that is so neuralgic in our country. But I had to bring it up, if for no other reason than to be truthful about what it means to be an image of God. Each of us needs to speak honestly with God and with one another about what to do with this issue.

I would like to point out some instances when nonviolence was tried on a fairly large scale with good, even if short-term, results. In India, Mohandas Gandhi organized large numbers of fellow Indians to protest nonviolently against British rule. Eventually Britain conceded freedom to

India. Gandhi tried to keep Hindus and Muslims together in one country but failed; the subcontinent was divided into a predominantly Hindu India and a predominantly Muslim Pakistan. Predictably these two countries face one another as enemies to this day.

In the United States, Martin Luther King Jr. fostered a nonviolent movement against racial segregation in the 1960s and 70s. The movement was extraordinarily successful in bringing together African Americans and white Americans to protest nonviolently against African Americans being forced to eat at segregated lunch counters, to ride on segregated buses, and so on. King wanted his followers to live as if the Peaceable Kingdom were already here. In other words, they tried to do what all Christians are called to do since the resurrection of Jesus: to live as if the new creation begun by Jesus were already here, which, in fact, it is, although not completely. These followers of King became the Beloved Community desired by God. This movement did lead to the signing of the Civil Rights Acts of 1964 and 1968 by President Lyndon B. Johnson. Unfortunately, laws alone will not erase racial injustice, as we have seen in the United States in the years since. Only a change of hearts and minds will make us into something close to the Beloved Kingdom.

The dissolution of the Soviet Union in 1991 came about gradually as the people of the countries absorbed by that Union displayed their disillusion through mostly nonviolent protests. The president of the USSR, Mikhail Gorbachev, signed the agreement dissolving the Soviet Union and forming a confederation of independent states in 1991. Then Gorbachev resigned and handed over the presidency of the Russian Federation to Boris Yeltsin. The world was amazed that the dissolution came so quickly and without any violence. However, again the euphoria was short-lived as the Russian Federation gradually devolved into what is once again a totalitarian state, causing friction in that part of the world and elsewhere. Unless hearts and minds are converted, I'm afraid, we will not have the Peaceable Kingdom.

The fact that all three of these examples did not achieve all that was originally hoped for reminds us that we are all sinners, all of us, and that any instance of the beloved community is in danger not because of "them," but because of "us." Remember Pogo's statement: "We have met the enemy, and he is us."

How do you react to this section? Do you want to have a conversation with God about the issues raised? I hope that together we can come up with ways forward for reducing violence in our country and in our world.

Our Planet

The last issue I want to raise for consideration is our relationship with our planet. More and more of us are realizing how precarious life on our planet is becoming because of global warming. Pope Francis's encyclical *Laudato Si'* has made clear that care for our planet is a serious responsibility for all of us. In fact, as we have seen from the beginning of this book, God wants our friendship and cooperation in caring for everything that exists. Everything in our universe, we are beginning to understand, is connected, so that what happens in one part affects the whole in some way.

We humans have often forgotten this fact and acted as though whatever we did was fine as long as no *person* was hurt. As we now know more and more clearly, this attitude has led to devastating results for our planet. I don't think I need to belabor this point. I presume that you are as aware as I am of how global warming, which threatens to destroy our planet, is caused primarily by human excesses. What I want to do here is raise the question of how we respond to our responsibility, as conscious images of God, to care for the very environment upon which our existence and the existence of all other species depend.

Once again, note that our actions can move events toward either decline or development, that we can participate in these cycles. Other creatures just do what comes naturally; we must choose how to act. God wants us to act for the good not only of humanity but also of the planet.

I suggest that all of us need to engage in a prayerful inventory of how we affect our environment for good and for ill. Let's take a stab at such an inventory now. This will be only a start since you will, I'm sure, come up with many more items than I do.

As we begin, let's ask God's help to look at our use of the goods of this world. Do we take for granted the water we drink and the food we eat? On this planet, millions cannot be sure of clean water and good food. And if we continue on our present path, water and food may well become so scarce that wars will be fought over them. Do we try to conserve water and not waste food? How about our use of energy? For light, heating, air conditioning, travel, etc.? Does our community offer ways to recycle materials that we might, without thinking, just throw away? Do we participate in that recycling? If no recycling is offered, do we press community leaders to begin it? I could go on, but I think it would be better if I left the rest to you.

We human beings are, I believe, on the threshold of a sea change in the history of our planet. If we continue to do business as usual, we are headed for disaster for our country and our world. All of us need to step up to the plate and do our best. Remember the words of Jimmy Dunne of the Sandler O'Neill corporation on why he and his company acted as they did after so many of the employees were murdered on September 11, 2001: "Because I knew that how we conducted ourselves in those first few hours and days would define who we really were and what we were about." How all of us act in this critical time for our planet will define who we really are and what we are about. Will what we do show that we are images of God or not? To answer that question in the affirmative will require that most of us move out of our comfort zones. But remember, even if doing so is frightening, God is with us. All we have to do is our small part in fostering the cycles of development God has already started in our world.

How do you react to this section? Whatever your reactions and thoughts, you can bring them into your ongoing conversation with God. What I want to leave you with is this: our actions as individuals and as communities do affect the universe for good or ill. As far as the future of our planet goes, we can be agents of decline or of development. God wants us to be agents of development. We can join God, with joy and hope.

A Practical Suggestion

I had finished the manuscript of this book, and it was already in the hands of Loyola Press, when the Jesuits of the United States and Canada published *Contemplation and Political Action: An Ignatian Guide to Civic Engagement*. I was delighted to see it and to realize that this was a gift of God for those who have followed my meanderings thus far in the book. After an introductory letter from Timothy Kesicki, SJ, President of the Jesuit Conference of Canada and the United States, and a prayer, the reader is invited to do what we have been doing in this book, but this time with a focus on how we can engage in political action as people who are called to cooperate with God in building up the kingdom of God. Readers are encouraged to engage in this prayerful reflection and to engage in discussions of the fruits of that reflection in groups with the hope that more and more of us will be moved to follow the advice of Pope Francis: "A good Catholic meddles in politics."[17]

Conclusion

I realize that I have touched on many issues in this chapter. I want to end it, however, with this reminder. Jesus proclaimed a God who did not impose impossible burdens on people. Given the enormity of the problems we face as individuals and as a people, we might be tempted to give up and leave all of them to someone else. Remember that, though precious in God's eyes, we are able to contribute only a small bit to God's immense creative work. In one of the most consoling of his words in the Gospels, Jesus said,

> Come to me, all you that are weary and are carrying heavy burdens, and I will give you rest. Take my yoke upon you, and learn from me; for I am gentle and humble in heart, and you will find rest for your souls. For my yoke is easy, and my burden is light. (Matthew 11:28–30)

Whenever you begin to feel overwhelmed by what you think are the requirements of being an image of God, remember these words. Remember, too, how, in chapter 6, we saw that the beatitudes are really about being happy: "happy are the poor," and so on. Jesus wants us to be happy and promises that we will be if we act as images of God. Becoming one of God's protagonists in the grand story of this world, cooperating with God, whom we love, should give us deep joy even if we must face ridicule or rejection from those who do not agree with our way of speaking and acting.

Epilogue

As we come to the end of this book, let me give you an example of how God's love transformed a place that is almost the epitome of evil in the modern world: Auschwitz, site in present-day Poland of the former Nazi death camp. In *One Long River of Song*, Brian Doyle has an essay called "The Lair." In it he tells a story he heard and never forgot about something that happened to a group of western Buddhists who stayed in the ruins of Auschwitz and other death camps for a week at a time. The story was told by one of the participants, identified in a footnote as the deceased novelist Peter Matthiessen. The group spent the week walking around, weeping, sitting for long periods of time in prayer, and walking through the museums. Doyle writes what Matthiessen said about one evening.

> One night at Auschwitz, he said, we were all gathered together in one room, more than a hundred of us, when a rabbi with us reached out with both hands and grasped the hands of the people standing next to him. Slowly most of the people in the room began to hold hands, and then they began to sway a little, and then some began to gently dance, and then, he said, there rose up in that room such a powerful joy that we were stunned and speechless and confused. Nearly every person in that room felt that sweeping joy, he said, but not everyone; several people ran out, horrified that there was joy here at the very heart of evil.[18]

The storyteller tried to make sense of what happened, even writing a novel that fictionalized the event. Here is my take on it. I believe that God is never absent anywhere in this universe. God was present in Auschwitz, not just when this group was there but while the evil unfolded. There have been numerous accounts of how, even under these appalling conditions, people acted as images of God, helping others, for example, and even giving up their lives for the sake of others. I believe that God was present even in this hell on earth, working to transform evil into good through love. This group of Buddhists were immersed in the memories of the horrors that seemed to permeate that place, but as they suffered in compassion for those who were imprisoned and killed there, they felt God's presence, moved, no doubt, by holding hands and swaying together. I would say that they were "surprised by joy," to borrow the title of the book by C. S. Lewis.

God is love, no doubt. But God is also joy, an unimaginable joy we sometimes experience when least expecting it. Evil did not have the last word at Auschwitz; love did. And this group of friends of God, who went to Auschwitz out of compassion and, perhaps, because of a sense of being called there together, experienced God's joy and love. Perhaps, too, the joy they experienced was something akin to Jesus' joy when resurrected.

Does that make sense to you? It's a great mystery. There is and has been so much evil in the world that it is hard to believe that love does and will transform evil. Sometimes, as in the depths of what looks like the triumph of evil, people experience a mysterious, joyful, and surprising love that conquers all. Julian of Norwich seems to have had such an experience during the Black Death (bubonic plague) in Europe and when she herself seemed about to die. She survived and afterward wrote an account of her visionary experience in which this line occurs: "And all shall be well, and all manner of thing shall be well." Have you ever experienced anything like this?

As we near the end of this journey, I want to remind you of Jesus' parables of the mustard seed and the yeast. Let's read them together prayerfully.

> He put before them another parable: "The kingdom of heaven is like a mustard seed that someone took and sowed in his field; it is the smallest of all the seeds, but when it has grown it is the greatest of shrubs and becomes a tree, so that the birds of the air come and make nests in its branches."
>
> He told them another parable: "The kingdom of heaven is like yeast that a woman took and mixed in with three measures of flour until all of it was leavened." (Matthew 13:31–33)

We who are conscious images of God are asked to act like the mustard seed and the yeast. We are asked to believe that we are important to God's dream for our world but to remember that we are just little seeds in God's great garden. We do what we can to be images of God in this world and leave the rest to God. God, by creating the world as it is, has become dependent on us to be that seed, that yeast. I wrote this book to help you as best I could to accept God's offer of friendship with its corollary of cooperating with God in his dream of a world that is the Peaceable Kingdom. We don't have to do the heavy lifting. God will take care of that. But if we want to be happy and if we want to be human beings, we need to act as images of God during our short time on this earth and thus give God joy *and* be a bit of the yeast that moves our world toward the Peaceable Kingdom. God begs us not to let the enormity of the task God is engaged in deter us from doing our small part. Let's contribute to God's joy.

I am encouraged by something the Christian historian Herbert Butterfield wrote about love and nonviolence many years ago.

> Here is the last safety-valve that Providence offers within human history itself, when the forces of evil seem to have sealed up the outlet to any other hope. When power is at its most implacable and self-righteousness is at its stiffest there is an extreme point where only Love can still fight and it can only fight with the weapons of non-resistance. . . . Somewhere there is a callousness that becomes unfrozen by the challenge of so much Love coming into the world only to meet with Crucifixion. . . .
>
> The role of Christianity in history has been most impressive when it has followed this pattern—not when it has been self-righteous or denunciatory but when it has been patiently drawing men with cords of love, and has sought no power except that which comes from its very powerlessness. Where Christian wisdom has most excelled all kinds of worldly wisdom even in the conduct

> of mundane affairs has been in the cases where it has relied on love, and that perhaps is why the lives of saints seem more efficacious in history than the decrees and the pontifical judgments of ecclesiastics.[19]

Finally, I ask you to read prayerfully what Paul writes to the Philippians. I would ask you to imagine that God, rather than Paul, is speaking these words directly to you. Read it slowly and prayerfully.

> If then there is any encouragement in Christ, any consolation from love, any sharing in the Spirit, any compassion and sympathy, make my joy complete: be of the same mind, having the same love, being in full accord and of one mind. Do nothing from selfish ambition or conceit, but in humility regard others as better than yourselves. Let each of you look not to your own interests, but to the interests of others. Let the same mind be in you that was in Christ Jesus,
>
> who, though he was in the form of God,
> did not regard equality with God
> as something to be exploited,
> but emptied himself,
> taking the form of a slave,
> being born in human likeness.
> And being found in human form,
> he humbled himself
> and became obedient to the point of death—

even death on a cross.
Therefore God also highly exalted him
and gave him the name
that is above every other name,
so that at the name of Jesus
every knee should bend,
in heaven and on earth and under the earth,
and every tongue should confess
that Jesus Christ is Lord,
to the glory of God the Father.
(Philippians 2:1–11)

From the beginning of creation God has been imploring us humans to give God this joy, to see us as reveling in the privilege of being like God. This book has been about helping all of us give God that joy by doing the sometimes hard work of cooperating with God in the unfolding story of creation, conflict, redemption, and grace.

Amen.

Acknowledgments

No one writes a book alone. That's for sure. I want to thank God, first of all, that this book came into my thoughts and that, at every roadblock, (and there were many) I was given a way forward. As usual I thank my sisters, Peggy, Mary, and Kathleen, for their unfailing love and care for me over almost ninety years. My dear friend Marika Geoghegan encouraged me through the whole time of writing, and especially when I was stymied.

I have dedicated the book to my six nieces and nephews and their families. I have had the privilege of knowing and loving them all their lives. I baptized all but one of them; Mary Beth was born a few months before I was ordained. I was the celebrant at their weddings and baptized their children. I delight in seeing them, which, unfortunately, is not often enough since they now live in the Midwest and I am an old man. But I feel blessed that I can dedicate this book to them. They are all wonderful human beings.

I am deeply grateful to Ligita Ryliškytė, SJE, whose dissertation gave me the inspiration for this book. In addition, she read a draft of the manuscript, assured me of my grasp of one of her main points, and gave me invaluable comments to enhance its contents.

Six good friends read the whole manuscript and made invaluable comments that have improved the book immensely; they are Carol Johannes, OP; James Martin, SJ; Pam McCormick; William C. Russell, SJ; Simon E. Smith, SJ; and Judith Talvacchia. I am very grateful to all of them. Bill Russell did more than just read and critique the manuscript; he also listened to me daily, especially when I was struggling with how to proceed. He is the epitome of what a friend and brother in Christ should be.

I thank my spiritual director, Ellen Keane, SND, a wonderful listener who asks judicious and insightful questions and is always encouraging and challenging.

I started writing this book as the COVID-19 pandemic forced a lockdown of Campion Center, where I live. Since part of this center is a nursing home, we were closed to outside visitors and also limited to our grounds. More than at any other time I can remember, we Jesuits were limited in our contacts with the world outside our home for five months and counting as I write. We have weathered the time together remarkably well, thanks to the grace of God and to the good will of all of us. I am very grateful to my brothers in Christ here at Campion Center.

Of course, our community has been sustained by an incomparable staff who have themselves stayed healthy, for the most part, and have kept us healthy. The staff here is extraordinary in their dedication to caring for us, each in his or her own way, and in doing this with love and humor and professionalism. Hats off to the staff at Campion Center.

Finally, many thanks to Loyola Press, especially editor Vinita Wright, for publishing so many of my previous books and now helping me give this "last book" to the world.

Loyola Press would like to thank Fr. Jim Martin, SJ, who stepped in for Fr. Barry after his death, to help us complete this book's final stages.

Endnotes

1. Krista Tippett, *Becoming Wise: An Inquiry into the Mystery and Art of Living* (New York: Penguin Books, 2017), 110–11.
2. W. H. Vanstone, *The Stature of Waiting* (New York: Morehouse Publishing, 2006), 95–96.
3. W. H. Vanstone, quoted in James M. Watkins, *Creativity as Sacrifice: Toward a Theological Model for Creativity in the Arts* (Minneapolis: Fortress Press, 2015), 217.
4. Rodney Stark, *The Rise of Christianity: How the Obscure, Marginal Jesus Movement Became the Dominant Religious Force in the Western World in a Few Centuries* (New York: HarperCollins, 1996), 6.
5. Paul Johnson, *The History of Christianity* (New York: Touchstone, 1976) quoted in Rodney Stark, *The Rise of Christianity*, 84; grammar is as cited.
6. Stark, *Rise of Christianity*, 213.
7. Stark, *The Rise of Christianity*, 211.
8. Stark, *The Rise of Christianity*, 215, italics in original.

9. Rodney Stark, *The Rise of Christianity: How the Obscure, Marginal Jesus Movement Became the Dominant Religious Force in the Western World in a Few Centuries* (New York: HarperCollins, 1996) (New York: Harper Collins, 1996), 215, italics in original.

10. Rabbi Zalman Schachter-Shalomi, *From Age-ing to Saging* (New York: Warner Books, 1995), 118.

11. Franz Wright, *God's Silence* (New York: Alfred Knopf, 2006), 41.

12. Brian Doyle, *One Long River of Song* (New York: Little, Brown and Company, 2019), 168–69.

13. Brian Doyle, "The Children of Sandler O'Neill" in *Eight Whopping Lies and Other Stories of Bruised Grace* (Cincinnati, OH: Franciscan Media, 2017), 145.

14. Rutger Bregman, *Humankind* (New York: Little, Brown and Company, 2019), 33.

15. Kate DiCamillo, *Because of Winn-Dixie* (Somerville, MA: Candlewick Press, 2000), 126.

16. Krista Tippett, *Becoming Wise: An Inquiry into the Mystery and Art of Living* (New York: Penguin Books, 2017), 236.

17. You can download this twenty-page guide from the website for the Conference of Jesuits of Canada and the United States, https: //www.jesuits.org/wp-content/uploads/2020/08/CivicEngagement-v10.pdf.

18. Brian Doyle, *One Long River of Song*, (New York: Little, Brown and Company, 2019), 172–73.

19. Herbert Butterfield, *History and Human Relations* (London: Collins, 1951), 53–55.

Works Cited

Bregman, Rutger. *The Guardian*. May 9, 2020. https://www.theguardian.com/books/2020/may/09/rutger-bregman-our-secret-superpower-is-our-ability-to-cooperate.

Brooks, Arthur C. *Love Your Enemies: How Decent People Can Save America from the Culture of Contempt*. New York: HarperCollins, 2019.

Butterfield, Herbert. *History and Human Relations*. London: Collins, 1951.

Doyle, Brian. *Eight Whopping Lies and Other Stories of Bruised Grace*. Cincinnati, OH: Franciscan Media, 2017.

Doyle, Brian. *One Long River of Song*. New York: Little, Brown and Company, 2019.

González, Antonio. *God's Reign and the End of Empires*. Translated by Joseph V. Owens. Miami: Convivium Press, 2012.

Green, Joel B., ed. *The CEB Study Bible*. Nashville, TN: Common English Bible, 2013.

Kochems, Timothy. "Raveling the Thread of a Therapist." *Voices*, Spring 2020.

Matthew, Iain. *The Impact of God: Soundings from St. John of the Cross*. London: Hodder and Stoughton, 1995.

Ryliškytė, Ligita, S.J.E., *Cur Deus Cruciatus? Lonergan's Law of the Cross and the Transpositions of "Justice over Power"*. A dissertation submitted to the faculty of Theology Department in partial fulfillment of the requirements for the degree of Doctor of Philosophy, Morrissey College of Arts and Sciences, Boston College, March 2020.

Stark, Rodney. *The Rise of Christianity: How the Obscure, Marginal Jesus Movement Became the Dominant Religious Force in the Western World in a Few Centuries*. San Francisco: HarperSanFrancisco, 1996.

Tippett, Krista. *Becoming Wise: An Inquiry into the Mystery and Art of Living*. New York: Penguin Books, 2017.

Vanstone, W. H. *The Stature of Waiting*. New York: Morehouse Publishing, 2006.

Wright, Franz. *God's Silence*. New York: Alfred Knopf, 2006.

Wright, Nicholas Thomas. *Matthew for Everyone*. Louisville, KY: Westminster John Knox Press, 2004.

About the Author

William A. Barry, SJ, devoted his life to the spiritual nurturing of others, through various roles in the Jesuit community and also through his many decades as a spiritual director and retreat leader. His many books, including *A Friendship Like No Other* and *An Invitation to Love*, have helped people pray, learn about faith, and deepen their friendship with God. Fr. Barry died in 2020, at age ninety.

MORE BOOKS BY **WILLIAM A. BARRY, SJ**

Experiencing God in the Ordinary

Experiencing God in the Ordinary will help you discover through prayer and meditation that God is always present and can be found in an ordinary day.

PB | 978-0-8294-5033-0 | $14.95

An Invitation to Love

In *An Invitation to Love*, Father Barry provides personal, adaptable retreat sessions/reflections focused on the concepts of love for God and neighbor—the great commandment.

PB | 978-0-8294-4667-8 | $14.95

Praying the Truth

Praying the Truth helps us deepen our friendship with God by examining how to approach God, at any time and with any problem, in complete honesty.

PB | 978-0-8294-3624-2 | $14.95

Changed Heart, Changed World

In *Changed Heart, Changed World*, Father Barry delves into such topics as how friendship with God impacts our role in society, how to see forgiveness as a way of life, and how compassion and a changed heart can change the world.

PB | 978-0-8294-3303-6 | $14.95

TO ORDER: Call **800.621.1008**, visit **store.loyolapress.com**, or visit your local bookseller.